BROTHER AGAINST BROTHER

Experiences of a British Volunteer in the Spanish Civil War

FRANK THOMAS

Edited by
Robert Stradling

SUTTON PUBLISHING

First published in the United Kingdom in 1998 by
Sutton Publishing Limited · Phoenix Mill
Thrupp · Stroud · Gloucestershire · GL5 2BU

British Library Cataloguing in Publication Data
A catalogue record for this book is available from the British
Library

ISBN 0 7509 1645 1

 ALAN SUTTON™ and SUTTON™ are the
trade marks of Sutton Publishing Limited

Typeset in 11/13 pt Bembo.
Typesetting and origination by
Sutton Publishing Limited.
Printed in Great Britain by
WBC Limited, Bridgend.

CONTENTS

PREFACE AND ACKNOWLEDGEMENTS

This book is an unexpected outgrowth from my study *Cardiff and the Spanish Civil War* (Cardiff, 1996). A series of accidents explain its generation and unusual format. Though Frank Thomas generously allowed me use of his memoirs in preparing the former book, I did not then imagine that he would entrust me with the task of preparing a fully edited version for publication. His initial uncertainty in considering such a project was perfectly understandable. Any person who sympathized with the Nationalist side during the Spanish Civil War was looked upon askance for two generations by those with an interest (whether or not professional) in politics and/or history. Moreover, in the public reckoning, and in a myriad written and spoken casual references, they were put down as 'Fascists', or – even more thoughtlessly – as 'Nazis'. It can be stated with confidence that nowhere on earth are the feelings which give rise to such expressions more solidly entrenched than in South Wales. Some two hundred Welshmen, overwhelmingly from the south-east and the coalmining valleys, went to Spain to suffer and sacrifice for the cause of the Spanish Republic. Thirty-five were killed.

However, just as historians eventually came to accept that Franco's regime lacked most of the essential ideological core even of Fascism, let alone of Nazism, they are now (yet more grudgingly) coming to the conclusion that a victory for the Republic may have led to a Spain which was 'democratic' only in the East European sense, which became familiar after 1945. This, of course, does not mean that the International Brigaders fought for a Stalinist Spain. But likewise, *mutatis mutandis*, it must be allowed that Frank Thomas did not fight for a Fascist Spain.

No more than others are scholars apt to change where the comfortable, almost generic, assumptions of interpretation are concerned. Academic culture, especially in the social sciences, has been so deeply influenced by the heritage of the Spanish Civil War that it is almost generically imbricated in the left-liberal discourse produced by that phenomenon, and the living spirit of anti-Fascism which continued to burn thereafter. Yet, for all their positive influence on humanity, these agencies have acted, in mostly unconscious ways, to censor information and limit interpretation concerning the European Right in the twentieth century. From my work in Ireland, with veterans of the O'Duffy Brigade, I know that men who went to Spain full of genuine idealism ended up being ashamed of their participation in the war, not only refusing to record their experiences for witnesses (historians, journalists) whom they justifiably mistrusted, but even hiding their 'misguided' past from their own families.

Having surmounted Frank Thomas' reservations, it was with trepidation that I embarked upon the task of finding a publisher. In accepting the challenge, Sutton Publishing, in their role as distinguished and assiduous publishers of military history, were certainly influenced by Frank Thomas' unique status as the last of his kind, but also by a sequence of military experiences which are utterly remarkable by any standards. I was hard at work in fulfilling their commission when I received an indirect communication requesting me to contact Mrs Elin Williams in Newport, Dyfed. Mrs Williams had read my Cardiff book, and was especially interested in what was said about Sid Hamm, the young International Brigader who died in the battle of Brunete. I had approached this story largely from the perspective of the Abse family, his close friends, and knew very little about its subject. Mrs Williams, to my astonishment, revealed that she was in possession of

Sid Hamm's diary covering the period of his service in Spain. She and her late husband, John, had been Sid's comrades in the Cardiff student cadre of the Communist Party in 1936. The diary, brought back anonymously from the battlefield, was left among John Williams' effects on his death a few years ago. Not long afterwards, Mrs Williams agreed to my proposal that it might be published.

Although the idea of setting these two accounts cheek by jowl seemed to me an obvious one, its actual achievement posed problems. Spain itself has now entered, partly also by accident, the final stages of its brilliant and peaceful accomplishment of a mature, modern democracy. Released at last by the events of 1995–96 – Ken Loach's magnificent film, *Land and Freedom*; the sixtieth anniversary of the outbreak of the war; and ultimately by the breakdown of the *'Pacto de Olvido'* (an unspoken agreement to keep the Civil War out of the political arena) during the 1996 General Election campaign – the ghosts of that desperate and brutal past are being confronted and exorcised. History must contribute fully to this process. If the historian has a social mission, it should be one of active irenicism. Though certainly not at all costs, the enabling of an understanding between cultures which are historically and violently opposed must assume a certain importance. This conviction led me to ask Frank Thomas to (as it were) share his book, the publication of which he has awaited this sixty years, with an opponent who has been for a similar period revered by many as a martyr. He readily agreed. I can only hope that readers who treasure the heritage of Sid Hamm will at least appreciate the spirit of this agreement.

Every word of the documents presented here was written sixty years ago, between the months of March and September in 1937. Both the authors were born in Pontypridd, capital of the coalfields, but both were brought to live in Cardiff as children, and may be reasonably regarded as Cardiffians. Both were middle-class products of the fine old Cardiff grammar schools. One was an eager would-be soldier, who went open-eyed into the fray, the other a convinced pacifist, who had only a dim apprehension of the consequences of his action. One received two days' basic instruction before being pitched into battle, yet came unscathed through many of the most dangerous actions of the war, and in being finally wounded, received indirectly his return ticket for home and safety. The other was given a thorough military training in almost every relevant aspect of battlefield technique, yet died within his first hour of encountering the enemy in battle. As Sid Hamm arrived in Spain, Frank Thomas was helping to fortify the village of Villanueva de la Cañada; ten weeks later, the latter was just arriving home in Cardiff, while the former was being shot down in the attempt to capture this same village. One of the texts is a conscious artefact, an extended narrative with moments of reflection; the other hastily jotted, staccato, discontinuous and repetitive, like the rattle of Morse code, immediate and receptive. Yet both are equally vibrant and honest testaments of experience, careless of correctness, whether of politics or the psyche.

My thanks go primarily to Frank Thomas and his wife Mary, for their patient collaboration and hospitality. I am grateful to Elin Williams and to Leo Abse for invaluable information, coupled with rigorous but stimulating criticism of my approach to the history of the Spanish War; and to Lance Rogers, who fought shoulder to shoulder with Sid Hamm, and on through all the great battles of the war, remaining still independent in mind and resilient in body. However, I must also acknowledge – indeed, emphasise – that the last-mentioned three witnesses have personal reservations about the ethical nature of the enterprise which this book represents. The first two have taken up my offer enabling them to make relevant statements inside its covers.

Thanks are also due to Kate Johnson of the Audio Unit of the Imperial War Museum, Tish Newland and her colleagues at the Marx Memorial Library, and Luke McKernan of the British Film Institute, all of whom extended expert and informed assistance. Jonathan Falconer, my commissioning editor, adopted from the start an affirmative approach to the project that invigorated my task immensely. Finally, as ever, my wife Helen gave her indispensable advice and practical support.

NOTE FROM
ELIN WILLIAMS AND
LEO ABSE

Elin Williams writes:

I was glad, at the time of publication of Rob Stradling's book on Cardiff and the Spanish Civil War, to provide him with bits of information on the year 1936, when, as a student in Cardiff, I was involved in both friendship and political activity with a group of young men 'and women. Three of our group volunteered for the International Brigade and were killed; namely, Alec Cummings, Gilbert Taylor and Sid Hamm. I was also able to hand to Dr Stradling the diary written by Sid Hamm on the battlefield.

However, I wish to disassociate myself from the attempt (to use his own words to me) 'to understand and explain both sides involved'. The Spanish 'Civil War' was not a civil war except at its inception. It became a rehearsal for the Second World War, a practice ground for German and Italian bombers. Those who joined the International Brigade were anti-Fascist young people from various countries. Those who joined Franco's army were Fascist recruits, in fact, if not in conviction. It is as simple as that.

I cannot be objective on this issue. For my generation emotions are still raw from the memories of that time. The Spanish War was not a football match, neither does it need a referee.

Leo Abse writes:

I believe 'relativist' approaches can be very dangerous in certain contexts. Inevitably, seeking to 'undemonize' demons, far from encouraging (as Rob Stradling hopes) 'irenic understanding between enemies', is in my opinion more likely to reactivate the original conflict. As the events around the 'historical' debate in Germany over the moral assessment of Nazism have shown, it most certainly does not lead the protagonists to ecumenical conclusions.

We must not be afraid to hate evil, or try to deny our hostility to it, smothering it in spurious and fashionable inclusive consensus politics or whitewashing 'reappraisals'. Nothing can undo the fact that the bombing of Guernica was the preliminary to the bombing of Cardiff; that's what we believed in the 1930s would come about and, whatever other errors we made, on that basic issue Sid Hamm and all of us kids were right.

NOTE
Every effort has been made to trace the copyright holder of the photograph of Peter Kemp on the second page of the plate section. The author and publisher apologise for any breach of copyright; this was not intended. Any further information on this picture will be gratefully received.

GLOSSARY OF SPANISH ACRONYMS AND TERMS

CNT – Confederación Nacional de Trabajo (anarchist workers' union)

CPGB – Communist Party of Great Britain

FAI – Federación Anarquista Ibérica (anarchist leadership group)

PCE – Partido Comunista de España (Communist Party)

POUM – Partido Obrero de Unificatión Marxista (Libertarian Communist Party, strong only in Catalonia)

PSOE – Partido Socialista de Obereros Españoles (Socialist Party)

PSUC – Partido Socialista de Unificación Catalana (Catalan Socialist-Communist Alliance Party)

SWMF – South Wales Miners' Federation ('the Fed')

TGWU – Transport and General Workers Union

TUC – Trades Union Congress

UGT – Unión General de Trabajo (Socialist Party trade union)

Pueblo – Any settlement of a certain size and roughly 2–5,000 inhabitants

Bandera – Battalion of the Foreign Legion (200–600 men)

Estado Mayor – High Command (Brigade or Division level)

Pelotón – Platoon (16–20 men)

Escuadra – Squad (3–6 men)

List of Maps and Illustrations

List of Plates

INTRODUCTION

The Volunteers

'The years 1914–45 were the most terrible in all of human experience. Any person alive today who was born around 1900 should be regarded as a survivor, and thus as an object of the greatest public interest. Such characters deserve to receive an official pension in return for dictating their memoirs, simply by reason of having lived through a sequence of catastrophes whose magnitude is unprecedented except by the fall of Rome or by the Mongol invasions.'[1]

These words, by his namesake and celebrated historian of the Spanish Civil War, might have been written with the main author of this book specifically in mind. Frank Thomas (hereafter FHT) was a participant in events which have, ever since, been among the most heavily laden with meaning and message for anyone with a political or ideological gene. On the night of 19 November 1936, FHT stood on guard at the deepest point of penetration of General Franco's army into Madrid, inside the wrecked shell of the Hospital Clínico in the university city. His battalion had fought its way to the capture of this huge building, taking part in some of the most ruthless and courageous assaults known to twentieth-century warfare, and losing in the process three-quarters of its effectives in dead and wounded. Republican Madrid, as is famously known, resisted, and FHT's side did not pass. One of the most potently divisive and definitive of all wars, profusely creative of myths and profoundly formative of our present political culture, was fought out to the bitter end. The Nationalist salient in Madrid was

1

surrounded on three sides by enemy positions which in some cases were less than a hundred yards distant – and things were to remain exactly thus until the end of the war, two and a half years later. The Left made Madrid into the supreme symbol of liberty in defiance of tyranny but the city finally capitulated, and Franco marched in. FHT had quitted Spain long since, disillusioned with his adopted masters, and uncertain about even the desirability of Nationalist victory. Indeed, except within Spain and in one or two nations of Iberian-America, the cause for which he had fought and bled became widely unpopular, at best seen as desperately misguided, at worst as a proverbial paradigm of political evil. In many ways, and emphatically in the long term, it was not the victors but the vanquished who overcame and were justified. The shell of Madrid occupied and ruled by Franco is no more but the Madrid of *no pasarán* has become eternal. Or perhaps, as some might term it, ubiquitous.

Franco's Welsh volunteer lives today in contented retirement in a Cardiff suburb, unconcerned – almost unaware – that he is a unique character in the modern history of Britain and Spain. He can be regarded as the last survivor of a tiny number of men from the United Kingdom, Hugh Thomas himself estimates it as barely in double figures, who volunteered to fight for the Nationalist cause in the Spanish Civil War.[2] Despite my familiarity with the basic elements of his story, I still wonder to set them down. In October 1936, ten weeks after the military uprising against the Second Republic in Spain and Africa, FHT set out from Cardiff for Spain determined to enlist in the Spanish Foreign Legion. He was then twenty-two years old. Like so many others (if you like, his 'opposites') who went to fight on the side of the Republic, FHT left home surreptitiously, without informing family or friends. Like most of the International Brigade volunteers, too, he knew little about Spain and hardly a word of Spanish. But in sharp contrast to them, he belonged to no political party and had no relevant contacts, either in Spain or at home, to help expedite his wishes. He therefore travelled alone, at his own expense, and in everything except the literal sense under his own steam. He arrived in

Burgos, administrative capital of Nationalist Spain, and duly enlisted in the famous (or notorious) *Legión Extranjera*, in Spain commonly called *El Tercio*. Within little more than a week after leaving Cardiff, FHT was in action as an ordinary infantryman in the columns of the Army of Africa, spearheading the final thrusts of General Franco's hectic advance on Madrid.

FHT was born in Pontypridd in the fateful year of 1914. His background was middle class, his father having moved, in the early years of this century, from rural Welsh-speaking origins and set up a successful wholesale food supply business. At that time, Pontypridd, at the head of the Rhondda valleys, was part of the bustling economic boom which was conditioning the development of south-east Wales. The town stood in relation to the Rhondda in much the same way as Cardiff stood to the greater hinterland in which Pontypridd was subsumed. That is to say, it, too, had achieved its material formation through the convenient provision of a range of goods and services to many smaller and more remote communities. It had a thriving bourgeois culture, while both class structure and class relations were being rapidly altered by the steady rise in real wages and the birth of consumerism. Yet at the same time (as its geographical position indicates) Pontypridd was almost totally dependent on the single industry of coalmining. The town was the headquarters of the South Wales Miners' Federation and, in contrast to Cardiff, a hotbed of left-radical politics.[3] Being brought up in the salubrious suburb of Lanwood, FHT was insulated as a child from the social realities and struggles which constituted what historians have generally regarded as the common heritage of the south Welsh people in our century. The international side of that heritage was to be drawn on in response to the war in Spain, and Pontypridd became the recruiting centre for the 150 or so miners who volunteered, under the aegis of the Communist International (Comintern) and via its subordinate local organizations, to fight for the Spanish Republic.[4]

However, when FHT was five, his father, whose business had been hit by the postwar mining slump, moved lock, stock and barrel to Cardiff. Frank attended Cardiff High School from 1925 onwards, his favourite subject being history, an interest which competed for attention, not without success, with rugby and cricket. He left school in 1931 with a good crop of credits in the leaving certificate. In partnership with an elder brother, Brinley, he was helped by their father to set up as a poultry farmer near Cowbridge in the Vale of Glamorgan, but this venture was aborted in 1935, after which FHT took employment directly in the family business as a travelling salesman.

He enjoyed the travelling part of this job but little else. Like so many youngsters of his time, he was an avid reader and filmgoer. Historical romance fired his imagination, and being a child of the year *par excellence* when Mars was in the ascendant, he was excited by deeds of derring-do on battlefields in exotic lands. His broad political attitudes were formed by the unashamed chauvinism of much literature produced then for male children about the British Empire. It will surprise no one who has read this far to learn that he was specially fond of the novel *Beau Geste*, which first appeared in 1925. P.C. Wren's bestseller influenced FHT's own style of writing to a palpable degree. He states today with absolute honesty (indeed, relish) that his main motive for going to Spain was a thirst for adventure and glory, a life as far removed from commercial travelling as could be imagined, and which he believed only the ranks of a foreign legion could satisfy. Yet at the same time, the occasion – if you like, the cause – for heroism and self-sacrifice had to be a worthy one. And in the 1930s the issue of ideology was unavoidable.

Mr Thomas senior was a longstanding Liberal supporter and admirer of Lloyd George – a figure whom FHT himself accepted without question as the greatest living Welshman.[5] But as he grew more independent-minded, the latter took to reading the *Daily Telegraph* and the *Daily Express*, hardly guardians of the mainstream liberal conscience, but rather respective organs of army and empire. He became a strong anti-Communist. In the summer of 1936, the experience of watching the early newsreels from the Spanish War reinforced FHT's feelings. The violent 'anarchy' of the Spanish revolution vividly (and deliberately) featured by cameramen and commentators outraged his ideals of order and family, while pictures of Franco's legionaries and Moorish troops touched exactly the right spring in his youthful fantasies.[6] Though neither a Fascist (in the sense of party membership) nor an active Christian (though his family were Calvinistic Methodists) FHT was convinced that International Bolshevism was the enemy of civilization and – as he put it to me – 'worth fighting against'. In 1979, he told Hywel Francis that, 'I'd always been rightwing in politics, [but] I wouldn't say extreme right wing'.[7]

However, FHT's father, when approached by a *Western Mail* reporter in November 1936, was apparently less circumspect.

> Frank has always been interested in Fascist political beliefs, but, more than that, he has been restless, unable to suit himself to everyday life. His models were men like one-armed Gen. Sutton and Gen. Smuts; men, he averred, who had done things in the world. His mind was always on politics, but I pointed out to him the need for earning one's living and took him into business with me. He was a good salesman, and gave us no indication of the turmoil in his mind until October 5. . . . The last we heard from him he was in Burgos as a private in the Foreign Legion. He repeated his assertion that he was going to make a name for himself as great as any of his heroes. He has always believed the Communists are to blame for the world's ills and that they should be exterminated. Franco has given him a chance. . . . This will make a man of him.[8]

Apparently, FHT's letters home had gone astray. Not long after this *Western Mail* story, his parents wrote to Burgos to seek reassurance about his situation, and received from Luis Bolín, Franco's publicity chief, the letter reproduced here.

In 1979, FHT recalled his youthful feelings: 'the notion of the Foreign Legion appealed to me from the Romantic point of view.'[9]

ESTADO ESPAÑOL

CUARTEL GENERAL DEL GENERALÍSIMO

OFICINA DE PRENSA

Salamanca 22 de enero de 1937

Mrs. G.H.Thomas,
"Fascadale", Bryngwyn Road,
Cyncoed. Cardiff.

Dear Madam

It is with great pleasure that I send you good news of your son Frank. Your letter to General Franco's Headquarters, dated Dec. 7th, was passed on to me, and although I immediately asked for news, some time has passed before they arrived owing to the movements of the Company to which he belongs. The letters to which he refers have doubtless gone astray in France, for the French Postal authorities are not too careful of letters posted in our territory.

Your son is well and happy, doing his duty, fighting for a great and good cause, and much liked by his officers and comrades.

Yours sincerely,

[signature]

(CAPTAIN)

The letter received by FHT's parents from Luis Bolín, Franco's publicity chief.

His experiences in the Spanish War gave Frank all (and more than all) of the adventure he craved, but very little of the fame. After he met two photographers, including a movieman, during the advance on Madrid, his pictures went around the world. His parents saw him in the *Daily Sketch* as well as the local *Western Mail*, and also received a version which appeared in the *Toronto Star*. But the film footage seems to have ended up on the cutting-room floor. By the time FHT got home, even middle-class opinion had turned sharply against Franco and his exploits had lost any premium. Though his own heart had gone out of the 'Cause', he did not forthwith retire from the fray. In August 1938, the Marchioness of Bute published an article in praise of Franco's Spain in the *Western Mail*, and was attacked in the correspondence columns by an ex-International Brigader, Thomas Evans of Kenfig Hill. FHT gallantly sprang to the defence of the lady of Cardiff Castle: 'As an ex-combatant I can confirm Lady Bute's statements.' Hoping to counter the effect of the bombing of Guernica and the plight of the Basque children on public opinion, FHT deliberately chose to focus his letter on the vexed question of air raids. 'I presume that the bombardment of Toledo, Talavera and Caceres by Republican aircraft, which I witnessed, were simply figments of the imagination.'[10]

To this day FHT has no regrets about his involvement in Spain. He rejects (on the one hand) any accusation of having been an ally of Nazism; and is not bothered (on the other) by charges of having been a mercenary – which, in the true spirit of Beau Geste, he regards as an honourable profession. (In both of these attitudes, as it happens, the present writer concurs.) FHT resembled numberless earlier crusaders and *conquistadores* in being inspired by a perfectly natural and ethically legitimate mixture of ambition and idealism. When he set out from Cardiff in 1936, Spain was to be his fame and fortune, and counter-revolution his just cause.

A few years after FHT's family moved to Cardiff from Pontypridd, the same odyssey was undertaken by that of Sidney Hamm (hereafter SH). If the former was comfortable (even prosperous) middle class, the latter seems to have been fixed towards the lower end of that category – though, perhaps with upwardly mobile aspirations. When SH was eleven he went to secondary school at Howard Gardens, which was not regarded as being in the same class academically as FHT's Alma Mater, Cardiff High. SH's schoolmate, Leo Abse, who became his closest friend when they were in their mid-teens (c. 1934), recalls that he had no great aspirations to learning, at least in the sense that had been adopted by British society. With SH, sport easily dominated the curriculum; that is, until he discovered politics, doubtless under Abse's influence. Just as it seems significant that FHT was born in 1914, so likewise it should be noted that these boys both came into the world during the Year of Revolution – 1917. Together, the friends founded the Cardiff United Youth Movement, under the aegis of the Labour Party, and threw themselves into organizing meetings, speeches, concerts and demonstrations in support of the great social causes of the day. Unemployment, means testing, rearmament, above all the threat of fascism, now loomed large in SH's idealistic consciousness.

In the summer of 1936, SH left school and enrolled as an engineering student in Cardiff Technical College. He was already a familiar visitor to the Abse household in Roath Park, where he became a favourite both with Mrs Abse and her youngest son, the fourteen-year-old Dannie.[11] SH enjoyed what would be called 'street cred' today in Dannie's eyes since he was able and willing to argue a case on sporting matters as well as those of current affairs. In later years, Dannie was to write affectingly about this influence and about the death of his young role model as a martyr for freedom and justice in Spain.

As the earliest entries of his diary reveal, SH responded quickly to the outbreak of the Spanish War in July 1936. By the time the new college term started he was already active on the students' Spanish Aid Committee in support of the Republic (which anticipated the forming of the official 'adult' body later in the year). He began to read

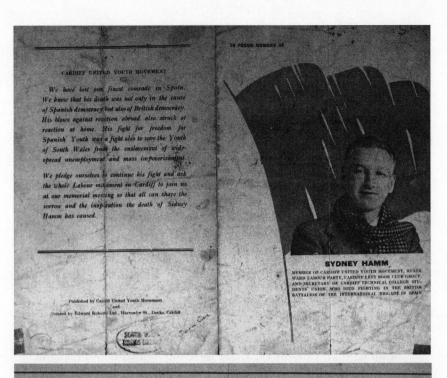

A leaflet published in memory of Sid Hamm.

political writings, and attended cultural events such as Left Theatre performances. In the winter of 1936–7, he became increasingly frustrated with the policy of Non-Intervention adopted by the Baldwin government and (in effect) endorsed by the opposition Labour Party. Doubtless he read reports of the massacre of militia prisoners at Badajoz in August, and was outraged by the photographs of children killed by Nationalist bombing at Getafe in October, as Franco's army closed on Madrid.[12] Though (of course) felt in an intensely personal way by each individual, the alteration undergone by SH was functionally identical to that being experienced simultaneously by thousands of men and women all over the world. Spain had provided the catalyst for a revolution in political perception, an epiphany which changed things utterly for large numbers of people who knew next to nothing about the country itself.

At some point early in 1937, SH took the step which so many of his contemporaries regarded as the logical one. Convinced that only the Soviet Union was committed to resisting international Fascism, he joined the Communist Party of Great Britain. He was clearly worried about the effect that this move would have on his best friend. Though subject to all the same influences of emotion and propaganda which had swayed SH, Leo Abse's political and cultural beliefs were too strong to allow him to embrace the Communism of Marx and Lenin. In this resistance, perhaps the sanctions of practical politics and the stirrings of political ambition also played their parts. At any rate, SH did not reveal his decision to the Abses, and (doubtless a contingent decision) did not leave the Labour Party. Nevertheless, he now moved in a different circle, in which he met students of the Young Communist League such as John Williams (later to be a prominent trades union lawyer) and Williams' future wife Elin Davies, along with older members of the movement, like Gilbert Taylor and Gerry Dooley.[13]

Not long afterwards, SH made the ultimate commitment and volunteered for the International Brigades. He was probably influenced by the plight of Madrid in the winter of 1936–7, the common cry of *no pasarán*, and the heroic defence of a sector of the Jarama front by the British Battalion in its baptism of fire in February. The appalling losses suffered then (many of them in direct combat against FHT's own unit) – though not revealed to rank and file loyalists back home – created an emergency need to rebuild the battalion's strength. Even before Jarama, its political commissar, Dave Springhall, had appealed to party secretary, Harry Pollitt: 'Why such an incredibly small percentage of comrades from South Wales? We could do with a group of 20–30 more of Welsh miner comrades. They, with their particular unity, singing and fighting qualities, would help to balance our battalion at present. Let us have some more of these in preference to the sort with no background at all.'[14]

Accordingly, SH was among a group of over twenty men, the largest single Welsh contingent, which left Cardiff on 17 April 1937. Party membership and personal eagerness had swayed acceptance since he only barely qualified on the socio-economic grounds prescribed by Springhall. Moreover, Leo Abse is concerned to this day by the fact that SH was accepted (along with two other Cardiff teenagers, Ken Widdess and Len John) when so few other volunteers from other parts of Wales were under thirty years of age at recruitment.[15]

At any rate, SH's group arrived safely in Paris, successfully evading the attentions of police invigilators on both sides of the Channel. They were now in the care of the large and well-organized French Communist Party. From this point, however, their route diverged from that normally taken by such expeditions. This usually led through obscure tracks across the Pyrenees to a general collection point at Figueras in Catalonia. SH, however, found himself in the fishing town of Seté in Languedoc awaiting transport by sea to Republican Spain. The reason for these contorted logistics lies in the bitter political divisions within the Republican camp. The quarrel between the dominant Socialist-Communist coalition and its main rivals, the CNT-POUM alliance, was reaching a critical stage. A little known consequence of this dispute was that, since the outbreak of hostilities, hundreds of pro-Republican foreigners attempting to cross into Spain via the Franco–Catalan frontier had been turned back, and some even imprisoned, by Anarchist militiamen manning the customs posts.[16] The celebrated 'secret trails' across the mountain barrier, patented by the Comintern, and which feature in the published accounts of so many veteran *Brigadistas*, were thus not so much a stratagem to frustrate the designs of Capitalist Non-Intervention (the usual explanation) as a manoeuvre intended to protect the forces of one Socialist-Republican faction against those of another.

When SH and comrades arrived in Barcelona at the end of April, they were at first taken to the Anarchist barracks. It seems unlikely that this was the result of a misunderstanding. The city was in a state of high tension, with mutual suspicions between the political sides reaching towards what was shortly to be a violent breaking point.[17] My reading of the diary entries from these two days suggests that SH and his group were deliberately detained by CNT members (*cenetistas*) as part of a situation in which both sides were manoeuvering for position. On 25 April, a leading member of the Communist PSUC was assassinated by Anarchist 'uncontrollables'. Worried that worse was to come, the Valencia government took certain moves – notable among these was the takeover of the frontier posts mentioned above, where incoming International Brigaders had in the past been detained by Anarchists.[18] With no Spanish nor Catalan, none of SH's group had much idea about what was happening, but in the circumstances they seem lucky to have escaped what would surely have been the status of hostages in the imminent armed struggle for the city and the ideological soul of the Republic.

SH survived the ambiguous threat of Barcelona – only to fall, nine weeks later, in the absolute context of the battle of Brunete. Meanwhile, in remarkable contrast to FHT, he had undergone intensive training in all aspects of contemporary infantry warfare. In May, when FHT, fighting near Toledo, received the injury which was indirectly to lead to his repatriation, some fifty kilometres to

the north the British Battalion was still in occupation of the
trenches which his comrades had failed to take in the last days of
the battle of Jarama. Despite this rigorous tour of duty, when they
were at last rested in mid-June, SH still had not actually sighted an
enemy. Instead, he was locked in a struggle with other hostile
elements. The diary reveals an obsession with his state of health; he
suffered an uninterrupted series of minor ailments, exacerbated by
wretched weather, worse food and general conditions of near-
exposure. The process of disillusionment was hastened by
incompetent authorities and dreadful discipline, the latter
characterized by a drunken rowdiness which constantly upset and
depressed him. His worries reflect little of the bullish morale often
claimed as the ruling atmosphere in more or less official
reminiscences. In late June, however, a welcome and enjoyable
furlough in Madrid seems to have lifted his spirits considerably.

A few days after SH's diary breaks off, the battle of Brunete
began. Perhaps, bolstered by his holiday, SH shared the sense of
confidence which apparently motivated the whole of the XV
International Brigade as it was launched in the van of this great
offensive, intended to entrap and destroy the Nationalist army of the
centre, while Franco was occupied on the northern front. On the
morning of 6 July 1937, SH's unit advanced from positions in the
Guadarrama foothills to capture the vital enemy position of
Villanueva de la Cañada. FHT had been stationed in this very place
for a blissfully peaceful week only a short while before, and spent his
duty hours in helping to improve its outlying defences.[19] His unit
then handed over to a battalion of *Falangista* troops, which was still
in residence when the Republican attack began.[20] FHT and his
compañeros had done a good job, and Villanueva was defended to the
death. We will never know if SH ever caught sight of the enemy.

One of several dozen Britishers killed in this engagement – and, in
fact, quite literally the victim of a Fascist's bullet – SH duly became a
martyr. In Cardiff, as was happening at intervals all over the country
(and in many other countries) the Communist Party arranged for the

appropriate rites of passage, *'pour encourager les autres'*. A memorial service was to be held at which various local political worthies would address the audience. Down from party headquarters in King's Road came the gifted orator, Isobel Brown, sometimes known as 'The English *Pasionaria*', to drive home the message that 'There can be no victory without sacrifice'. But SH's parents were very unhappy. Rather than celebrate their son's selfless achievement they were inclined to blame the Communist Party for his premature and needless death. In an attempt to get the meeting cancelled, they contacted the police. When he heard of their opposition, Leo Abse, who was due to speak, was placed in a difficult position. With her forceful charm, Isobel Brown persuaded the police to back off, and Abse felt obliged to carry out his appointed duty.[21] What followed is described in a memorable passage from Dannie Abse's semi-autobiographical novel. But the poet's memory (or imagination) lacked a certain degree of empathy when it came to describing his elder brother's comportment in the wake of the meeting.

> At last Leo shook hands with everybody, and stepped off the platform . . . I almost had to run to keep up with him. . . . All the time I was thinking . . . 'If I was bigger perhaps I could go to Spain. It was worth fighting for. Maybe if I got killed they'd have a memorial meeting for me' . . . Leo looked away. 'Non-intervention,' he laughed bitterly, 'non-intervention'. . . . 'If you feel so strongly about Spain,' I said, 'why don't you go there?' Leo gazed down at me from his 21-year-old eyes, as if he had been struck a blow.[22]

The document left by SH is quite unlike anything ever published before about the British Battalion of the XV International Brigade. It illustrates the rapid collapse in personal morale of the subject himself, taking place in a context where a collective morale seems to be conspicuous by its absence. By the time SH arrived at the Jarama front, a long (and almost unrelieved) period of trench-line duty had elapsed. Many men had lost close friends in the carnage of the Jarama battle (5–27 February); dozens more were in hospital with serious wounds; dozens more still were undergoing some kind of corrective detention after deserting in the face of the enemy on 12–14 February. The weather in that spring of 1937 was consistently dreadful, and by the early summer it was obvious that the war in the north, where Franco's troops had invaded the Basque country, was going badly for the Republic. In the circumstances, it is not surprising that the general spirit was low.

Undoubtedly, SH's strength of purpose was undermined by the fact that, within a few days of arriving at the training camp, his health began to suffer. Indeed, at times, the diary reads more like the obsessive moanings of a hypochondriac than the words of a young man who was known to his friends as an athlete as well as a political idealist. The level of drunken violence and general indiscipline deeply disturbed SH. Cynicism about his working-class comrades, and about the Communist cause, soon become evident. He refuses to volunteer for potentially dangerous duties, and after only one week at the front he is seeking repatriation. Diaries are by genre self-centred, but the absence of any mention of the Spanish people, their plight or their cause – even the routine phrases of outrage and solidarity which we often find in letters and memoirs – is striking. Yet this was no malingerer, adventurer, runaway delinquent or political subversive. SH came from what was (in the sense now appreciated by social historians) a 'respectable' family, and was a party member, who volunteered for Spain out of an overwhelming sense of commitment.

Of course, not all was grimness and depression. Even our knowledge of SH's tragic end should not be allowed to obviate those days when he felt a sense of delight and community with his comrades. These occasions were marked, above all, by music and singing – perhaps the most resonant medium of expression, which predictably and deeply moved all members of the Brigade (and, it must be said, those on the other side too) during this most terrible and most meaningful of all wars.

The Texts

FHT did not require the years and rewards recommended by Lord Thomas in order to commit his memoirs to paper. On returning to Cardiff from Spain, he began almost immediately to record his experiences, using one of the typewriters from his father's offices in Millicent Street. The book was completed by September of that same year, 1937. In this, also typical of his generation, FHT had always had an urge to write; a previously suppressed desire for a career in journalism was now brought to the surface by the injuries which he feared might incapacitate him for many other employments. At any rate, he consciously wrote his book with a view to publication.[23] There was another, perhaps less conscious motive in the act of composition. He was still in pain from the severe wounds suffered in an engagement near Toledo a few months earlier, and was often tormented by nightmares of horrific battle experiences, along with other brutal scenes, the consequences and accompaniments of a savage war, witnessed at first hand. The three months that passed in the writing process provided an effective therapy.

As it happens, those months were identical with the period in which George Orwell was writing *Homage to Catalonia*. Orwell – who fought with the pro-Republican POUM militia on the Aragon front, distant from the Madrid theatre – was seriously wounded by a Nationalist sniper during the same week that FHT was struck down by Republican bullets. Both men left Spain clandestinely and full of disillusionment about the cause for which they had risked their lives (June 1937). Exactly like Orwell, FHT kept a diary which went missing in the aftermath of injury and hospitalization. Once safely home, Orwell wrote the single most successful book ever to appear on the Spanish Civil War. Even within a bibliography greater than that devoted to any other war in history, *Homage to Catalonia* has enjoyed a quite unique popularity and influence.[24] In mundane contrast, FHT failed to attract the interest of any publisher (or indeed, any reader) for the manuscript of 'A Professional Soldier in

Spain'. When the great war against Fascism began in 1939, FHT joined up and his book was put away in a drawer, rarely to be taken out again.[25] In later years he came to realise that nobody cared to confess an interest in the memoirs of a fighter who had been on the 'wrong' side in Spain; this despite the fact that its author had fought against both Italian Fascists and German Nazis in North Africa, and had suffered another terrible wound during the retreat from Tobruk in 1942. Yet even here the resemblance with Orwell is not exhausted, for we must remember that Victor Gollancz, the left-wing publisher who had commissioned Orwell's book, rejected his manuscript because of its outspoken anti-Communist stance. Thus the comparative records of the most famous and (until now) the most obscure of memoirs on the Spanish Civil War represent a mutual journey to a kind of cathartic centre.

The ninety-four pages of text that make up 'Spanish Legionario' – some 31,000 words in all – are accompanied by three maps drawn freehand by the author.[26] These, like so much else in the memoir, impress by their sheer accuracy. FHT consciously decided to set everything down while recollection was still fresh. Not only did this impart dramatic immediacy to the description, and a stimulating (indeed, often overexuberant) vigour to the style, it also allowed him to record a wealth of personal, military and topographical detail. The main disadvantage to this procedure resided in the sometimes opaque and (relatively) disorganized nature of the narrative. Its subsequent history did not encourage the author to correct this situation, and the manuscript was never revised. However, in corroborating details with the works of the recognized authorities on the military campaigns of the Spanish Civil War – especially, but not exclusively, the work of Manuel Aznar and José M. Martínez Bande – I have found few serious discrepancies.[27]

Having 'lost' his diary (along with several other valuable mementos described in the memoir) FHT came back from Spain with little more than the clothes he stood up in. He had become reasonably fluent in Spanish but in those days before mass tourism few public libraries were well stocked with reference material (in any language) about the Iberian peninsula. To some extent, he was able to supplement his memory by collecting contemporary newspaper cuttings about the progress of the war. In any case, both in general and in particular, FHT demonstrates an acute capacity for observation. He evidently had a talent for strategy; perhaps inculcated by his interest in a subject (history) which was in those days mostly presented to young readers, both in and out of the classroom, in the context of national military glory, international rivalry and imperialist warfare. When he gives names and estimates numbers of units involved in any operation, he is invariably correct in the former case and as near the mark as makes no difference in the latter. In only one or two instances does he misspell the name of a Castilian town or village – some of the latter little more than obscure *pueblecitos* with a few dozen dwellings – which he visited in his travels. Moreover, his overall perception of the constantly developing military situation is impressive. True, during the writing process he acquired the thin layer of hindsight deposited by the great battles which took place after his return (Brunete in July–August 1937, and Teruel in December 1937–February 1938), but even so his grasp of the strengths and weaknesses of the Nationalist army's position on the Madrid front is astonishingly sound. Last but not least, like a good historian, FHT was very meticulous about recording his dates. On the whole, therefore, the editor has found that if the text has often required amplification and contextualization in the interest of the reader, it has only rarely demanded correction in those of scholarship.

Perhaps one of the most remarkable points to be made in this connection arises when FHT's recollections are compared with those of Peter Kemp, another British veteran of the *Tercio*. Kemp compiled his (much longer) memoirs twenty years later, and had ample opportunities to corroborate and verify the details provided by memory. As a volunteer, Kemp possessed other advantages not enjoyed by FHT. He was a highly educated and well-connected Cambridge graduate (in law). He served more than two years in the

Legion as an officer, having been personally recommended for this commission by General Millán Astray, following sterling service with the *Requetés*. In subsequent years he returned on various occasions to the peninsula, becoming familiar with Spain and its cultures. Yet one never derives from Kemp's (otherwise accomplished) book the clear, overall picture of the wartime strategic situation which FHT manages to impart from a considerably less privileged point of perspective.[28]

On the other hand, FHT's writing style – though appropriate, and often evocative, for a young and inexperienced writer – has its obscurities. These reside in a recurrent allusiveness to unrevealed familiarities, and occasionally confusing syntax. Here, usually as a result of consultation with the author, the editor has intervened with occasional slight emendations to the text, altering the arrangement of clauses in a sentence and (much less frequently) that of sentences in a paragraph. Some shorter paragraphs have been run together where felt appropriate, though without altering their sequence.

These stylistic questions took up a significant fraction of time spent in a series of eight interviews with the author, held in May and June 1997. FHT is eighty-three at the time of my writing this introduction; understandably, his memory of the events described in his book has faded into mostly vague shadows. Though now and again a new aspect of an event would be revealed in conversation, much more often nothing could be added, or else the incident in question was not remembered at all. During the original composition of the memoirs, despite growing scepticism about the Nationalist cause, FHT's opinions, and at times his mental pictures of empirical realities, were still moulded by the propaganda which had inevitably dominated his perceptions during his time in Spain. With his agreement, I have commented on one or two obvious instances thereof, purely in the interests of balance, and not with any desire to 'correct' matters, or any pretension to some objective 'truth'. FHT and I agree wholeheartedly that the secret of peace is compromise based upon understanding.

Though still convinced of the evils of applied Communism, the author has no personal bitterness towards any enemy with whom he fought in Spain. A cynic might say that this irenicism is a luxury that stems in part from having served on what was – even if in the highly conditional sense already referred to – the winning side. Ironically, however, given his desertion from its armed forces, the Francoist government would hardly have looked upon FHT with any more favour than an International Brigade veteran. For this reason, knowing as an old soldier that discretion was the better part of valour, he refrained from indulging in a Spanish holiday while Franco lived. As things worked out, the sheer longevity of his former *generalísimo* ensured that, in practice, he never has revisited the scene of his youthful exploits, and never possessed any incentive to keep up his spoken Spanish. Doubtless these exigencies have also helped to accelerate the fading of his memories of those savage and epic adventures.

In the case of SH's text, matters are somewhat more straightforward. As an original artefact, it occupies a college pocket diary (measuring the regulation 3.5 in by 2.5 in), bearing on its front cover the legend 'Cardiff Technical College, Students' Union, 1936–1937', and the arms and motto of the said institution. In the preliminary matter, the owner has entered his name and department (Handicrafts), and declared his interest in cricket, rugby and tennis. A curriculum timetable is drafted out on one of the blank pages, accompanied by some scribbled names and addresses.[29] It seems that SH was involved in the student rag early in 1936, and evidently helped to produce the proto-satirical newsheet entitled *The Wail*, which is remembered fondly by many Cardiffians of a certain age. Normally SH did not 'keep a diary' in the conventional (retrospective) sense. Indeed, he seems not to have needed one even in the alternative (prospective) sense. Not until well into 1937 – Sunday 19 March, to be exact – does he make the first entry, noting that there was to be a film show. Thereafter, scattered (mainly political) appointments crop up until the date in April when the sudden announcement is made of his departure for Spain.

Thereafter, and until it breaks off, equally abruptly, four days before his death, there is an entry for almost every date. These become more and more detailed, the handwriting gradually assuming minuscule proportions as the writer becomes more observant and involved with his task. Entries are made in telegrammatic style, the calligraphy is often not readily legible, and the order of events in any one day is sometimes difficult to establish.[30] I have noted as 'illegible' certain words or phrases which have obstinately resisted relevant translation; on far more occasions I have essayed a conjecture as to their content or meaning, drawing for this purpose on a knowledge of the history of the British Battalion derived from a wide variety of sources.[31]

The diary was never seen, and thus was never censored, by any political commissar. In this pristine state, it is a very rare and valuable record. According to Elin Williams, it was taken from SH's dead body on the battlefield, prior to his hasty burial in one of the shallow, unmarked graves evoked in the title of one veteran's memoirs.[32] One of the dead man's Welsh comrades took it home, and gave it to Mrs Hamm. At some later point, perhaps when grief and bitterness had subsided sufficiently, she passed it on to SH's closest associate in the Communist movement, the lawyer John Williams. The last entry (for Tuesday 6 July) was made by Williams, and states, 'On this day Sid Hamm was killed in Brunete, Spain'.[33] Following her husband's death a few years ago, Elin Williams became steadily more aware of the potential importance of this document. After reading my book on Cardiff and the Spanish Civil War, she contacted me and entrusted the diary to my care.

The Spanish Foreign Legion

The regiment in which FHT enlisted had come into being as recently as 1920, indeed, its first campaigns took place at the time that P.C. Wren was writing his famous novel about its French precursor.[34] Certainly, the Legion's creator, Lt-Col. José Millán Astray, was an admirer of the famous French outfit. With King Alfonso XIII's backing, he set up this new force and was appointed its first commander, though it was not built up quickly enough to prevent the humiliating Spanish defeat at Anual in 1921. After this setback, Millán Astray was joined by the ambitious young officer, Francisco Franco, who became his protégé. Together they forged a formidable weapon, which contributed decisively to final victory over the 'rebel' alliance in Morocco in 1927. In succeeding years (partly as a result of a comparative lack of action, and thus of demand) one of the main features of the *Legion Étrangère* was abandoned, and the Spanish version came to be made up not of foreigners, but mostly of native Spaniards dedicated to the army as a career, as distinct from mere conscripts. The key to its success was an utterly ruthless and selfish military professionalism, a *reductio ad absurdum* of the intensely proud self-regard of the Spanish army as a whole – or, at least, of the officer class, who regarded themselves as the ineluctable guardians of the soul of the nation, and thus above politics and conventional morality.[35] The Legion, in particular, had a sense of history being on its side, while each member was vowed to a self-abnegating, collective well-being. These features seem a bizarre reflection of the Marxist principles held by those who became their most effective adversaries on the field of battle in 1936–8. Millán dedicated his corps to reviving the spirit of the invincible infantry of the Army of Flanders in the time of the Spanish Habsburgs – the quasi-legendary *'Tercios'* of leaders like Alba, Spínola and Farnese.[36]

Millán Astray was a perfect role model for the young FHT. It is Millán's 'Credo', composed for the Legion in the 1920s, which he placed at the head of his book. At that time, he felt these nostrums represented an epitome of his own life as a professional soldier but in which he had been let down by the Legion itself. However, in the course of the war, Millán came to be identified with the most atavistic and mindless aspects of the Nationalist cause. A sinister and fantastic figure, appearing to modern view as a character out of Stephen King's imagination, the colonel had lost a leg, an arm and an eye in combat, while what remained of his piratical figure resembled nothing so much as a living skeleton. He and his more famous understudy had inspired a military ethic which was both reckless (in terms of personal safety) and ruthless (in terms of treatment of the enemy). He had given his Legion an aptly outrageous slogan, *'¡Viva la Muerte!'* ('Long live Death!'). The general's utterance of this cry during a dramatic assembly in Salamanca (shortly after FHT had passed through the city) moved Spain's greatest living intellectual, Miguel Unamuno, to turn against the Nationalist cause, which he had initially espoused as saving Spain from chaos. The incident took place in the *'aula de Luis de León'*, the most celebrated lecture theatre in Spain – arguably in all of Europe. As Millán shouted him down with yells of *'¡Muere la Inteligencia!'* ('Death to the Intellectuals!') the aged philosopher – who was also director of the university – was hustled from the hall. Shortly afterwards Unamuno died, doubtless as a result of the stress and emotion caused by this confrontation.[37] The Millán–Unamuno contest was quickly projected in Republican propaganda as symbolic in a way which robbed its enemy – rightly or wrongly, but definitively in the eyes of the liberal-intellectual world – of any claims to humanistic culture.

During the summer of 1936, the dynamic element of the insurgent war effort had been largely derived from the power of the Army of Africa. This approximately 17,000-strong force was based on eight battalions (*banderas*) of the Foreign Legion, along with various Moorish auxiliary units derived from the local tribes of Spanish Morocco. In the first ever military airlift (as the textbook commonplace has it) most of this army, now commanded by General Franco, was transported across the Straits of Gibraltar with the aid of four Junkers 52 aircraft, provided for the purpose by the personal decision of Adolf Hitler. From that moment the fate of the war rested on Franco's sword. In the north, General Emilio Mola had been highly successful, not only in coordinating the rebellion in various centres, but in establishing a solid core of insurgent territory. But though Mola captured some key points, his advance on Madrid was definitively halted by Republican resistance in the Guadarrama mountains north of the capital. Mola's somewhat

heterogenous forces, despite the presence of the fanatical Carlist
(*Requeté*) militias, lacked effective assault formations. This was
precisely what Franco's Legionaries and Moors provided.

Seven of the *Tercio's* eight *banderas*, mustering less than 4,000 men –
about 25 per cent of the whole *africanista* command – were transported
to the Seville–Cadiz region during the two months after the rising.
Following a plan of campaign worked out by Franco and the Legion's
field commander, Juan Yagüe, two of these remained behind to stiffen
the new (mainly conscript) army being raised to extend rebel control
over Andalusia, while the remaining five, and most of the Moroccan
units, advanced towards Madrid in two columns.[38] (The Sixth *Bandera*,
which FHT was to join a few months later, was one of the former.)
Great though the success of this operation was to be, it seems that, if
anything, its commanders were disappointed by their army's
performance. The opposition comprised huge but undisciplined
agglomerations of political party and trades union-based militia bands,
badly armed, worse disciplined, 'coming out from the towns as if to
hunt rabbits', as one contemptuous Nationalist officer put it.[39] In fact,
it was the hapless militiamen themselves who were the rabbits – often
almost literally if they were unlucky enough to fall alive into the hands
of the Moors.[40] Fighting in climatic and topographical conditions
which closely reproduced their normal theatre of operations in the
Mahgreb, Franco's columns at first swept all before them, capturing
huge swathes of territory and much of the enemy's equipment,
abándoned in a long series of disastrous routs.

Not until the town of Badajoz put up unexpectedly stout
resistance did Yagüe suffer his first significant losses (14–15 August).
Thereafter, however, as the columns moved into the Tagus valley for
the last lap, it seemed that each settlement in their path demanded a
higher price for capture. On 1 September the taking of Talavera de la
Reina (later to become the headquarters of the *Tercio*) was especially
costly. The government now strained every nerve to slow down the
rebel advance and provide time to prepare Madrid for the ultimate
resistance. Franco then (as many argue) offered Madrid, and the

Republic, a priceless breathing space by deciding to turn aside and relieve a small Nationalist force holed up since the outset of hostilities in the Alcázar (castle) of Toledo. In order to guarantee the success of this operation, his general staff demanded replacements for the hundreds of fallen *africanistas*; and at this point, the *Sexta Bandera* (under the Moroccan officer, Mohammed Ben Mizian) was called up from the south and allocated to the column commanded by Colonel Asensio Cabanillas, victor of Talavera. In the event, Toledo, a natural bastion, was defended with utter incompetence and fell to its assailants with comparative ease. Partly as a result of this prestigious triumph and having been appointed supreme commander (and Head of State), Franco paused in order to regroup and plan the final advance upon Madrid. It was towards the end of this period of hiatus that FHT arrived in Talavera and was allocated to the Sixth *Bandera*.

He had arrived at the opportune moment, since at this point a strong recruiting drive was under way to raise men for the *Tercio*.[41] Even the simplest calculations of potential casualties in the forthcoming assault upon the capital meant that, if left as they were, the *banderas'* depleted ranks would not last a week's fighting. Though, of course, the Nationalists were conscripting and training thousands of men of military age from among the (roughly) one-third of the Spanish population which they now controlled, such men could not be relied on to spearhead the kind of bloodily determined attacks which had become both necessary and routine. Only dedicated volunteers could be trusted to do the job in hand. As well as many Spaniards, hundreds of foreigners joined the Legion in 1936, coming from backgrounds, and acting for motives, just as varied as those of the International Brigades. The following pages introduce the reader to several characteristic individuals. Though the line is not always easy to draw, it remains broadly true that the fanatical valour of the *Tercio* stemmed from a purely military more than a strictly ideological ethic. Some, to be sure, were fanatical idealists, anti-Communist crusaders like the Rumanian group encountered briefly by FHT when sightseeing in Boadilla del

Monte.[42] Others, no less courageous as warriors, were mercenaries with little or no political motivation. Either way, they enjoyed privileged status in terms of pay and conditions, but lived according to an internal discipline which can only be described as ferocious.

Until the latter stages of the war, the presence of the Legion and that of their Moroccan auxiliaries (*regulares*) was a pre-requisite for any important Nationalist campaigns. As we shall see, by the time FHT decided to bow out, his *bandera*, in terms of its human constituents, was a virtually new and different outfit from that which he had joined six months earlier. Despite his strictures on the comportment and morale of the new generation, they were subsequently to distinguish themselves further on the northern front against the Basques, during the Teruel counter-offensive, and finally in the last great battle of attrition in the valley of the Ebro (July–September 1938), where the Sixth *Bandera* came for a second time directly up against the British Battalion of the XV International Brigade.[43] In the Civil War as a whole, the *Tercio* suffered the enormous number of 37,393 casualties, including 7,645 dead – the latter figure being almost twice that of the original muster of the regiment at the beginning of hostilities. The corps still serves the democratic Kingdom of Spain as garrison troops in its bizarre Gibraltar-like outposts at Ceuta and Melilla on the North African coast; but their last military action took place during the colonial war in Záhara (Spanish Sahara) in 1970–6.[44]

The International Brigades

Organized worldwide by the Comintern (the Third International, controlled by Stalin), there were a total of five brigades. The British Battalion (16th, later 57th) belonged to the XV Brigade, and was subdivided into four companies.[45] When SH arrived in Madrigueras, a village to the north of Albacete which was the British training billet, the pace of recruitment was at its most intense. Around twenty men were arriving every week, many of them reacting to the immediate stimulant of the bombing of Durango and Guernica by the Nazi Condor Legion. The battalion itself was still on active service on the Jarama front. Here, two months earlier, during a horrendous engagement and with astonishing courage, they had prevented Colonel Asensio's column from breaking through to the town of Morata, and thence to the Valencia road, Madrid's lifeline. SH was duly moved up to these trenches once his training was complete. Just before the battle of Brunete the battalion reached its optimum size of 640 men. Four weeks later less than a quarter of that number were still in the line.[46]

Other British volunteers served with Brigade units, such as the anti-tank company, communications, medical services and so on. The XV Brigade fought with enormous credit in every major campaign of the war, except that of the 'Basque' front. The International Brigades as a whole were among the most reliable regiments of the Republican army – especially important during the defence of Madrid in the winter of 1936–7. By the autumn of 1937, however, native Spaniards began to outnumber foreigners in all battalions, as the casualty rate climbed higher and the tempo of recruitment sank lower. In the autumn of 1938, Republican Prime Minister Negrín ordered their withdrawal as part of an agreement by which the Italian interventionist army (the CTV) was also withdrawn. Appropriately enough at the time of this agreement they were still fighting on the Ebro front, and (even more characteristically) were actually called back into the line to cope with an emergency after having been 'finally' withdrawn in accordance with it.

Since then, the capacity of their veterans for dramatic comebacks in many fields of endeavour has been a hallmark of their resilience. On the occasion of their stand-down march in Barcelona (October 1938), the celebrated Communist leader, Dolores Ibárruri, pleaded with the women and children of Spain never to forget them, and with the volunteers themselves to return to Spain one day when real peace had also returned. These words remained unheeded by the vast majority of Spaniards until in 1995 the National Parliament (Cortes) voted unanimously to offer the formal rights of Spanish citizenship to all surviving veterans. In November 1996, nearly 400 members of the worldwide I.B. Associations were welcomed to Spain for a week-long fiesta of remembrances and emotional expressions of appreciation.[47] As *La Pasionaria* prophesied, the International Brigades became history and legend, the most famous (and thus most influential) army defeated in the cause of freedom since that of Leonidas at Thermopylae.

Notes to Introduction

1. 'Los anos 1914–1945, la primera mitad de este siglo, fueron los mas terribles en toda la experiencia humana. Cualquier persona hoy viva, y nacida hacia 1900, deberia ser contemplada como un sobreviviente del maximo interes, digna de recibir una pension, simplemente para que dictara sus memorias, por la sencilla razon de haber vivido toda una secuencia de catastrofes de cuya magnitud solo hay precedentes en la caida de Roma o los invasiones de los mongoles.' H. Thomas, 'La guerra civil española en la historia', in R. Tamanes (ed), *La guerra civil española – una reflexíon moral, 50 años después* (Planeta, 1986), p. 66.

2. See H. Thomas, *The Spanish Civil War*, (3rd edn, Harmondsworth, 1977) p. 980. This estimate of their numbers calls for slight revision. For example, a survey of the wartime records of the Nationalist Foreign Office yielded several new cases; Ministerio de Asuntos Exteriores, Madrid, Archivo de Burgos, Carpeta R1059.

A *New* South Walian, Nugent Bull, also served in the Spanish Foreign Legion, the only one of sixty compatriots in Spain who joined the Nationalists. Some 2,100 British citizens (including medical personnel) served in Republican military units. Using the Australian percentage (1.666 rec.) gives a notional figure of thirty-five British volunteers on the other side. See J. Keene, 'An Antipodean Bridegroom of Death: An Australian Volunteer in Franco's Forces', *Journal of the Royal Australian Historical Society* 70 (1985), pp. 251–70. Bull was a flamboyant character who inherited an undertaking business and 'left his mark on the funeral industry in Sydney'. Ms Keene does not comment on the aptness of this background for a 'bridegroom of death' in an organization whose watchword was 'Long live Death'. (Bull died fighting with the RAF in the Second World War.)

There was also at least one other 'old' South Walian who aspired (apparently in vain) to enlist with Franco: see R. Stradling, *Cardiff and the Spanish Civil War* (Cardiff, 1996), pp. 46 and 129. However, given a sixty-year lapse, and the negative pressures still active in the cultural legacy left by the war, it seems unlikely that previously unknown veterans will ever reveal themselves.

3. H. Francis and D. Smith, *The Fed: A History of the South Wales Miners in the Twentieth Century* (London, 1980); C. Williams, *Democratic Rhondda: Politics and Society, 1885–1951* (Cardiff, 1996).

4. See H. Francis, *Miners against Fascism: Wales and the Spanish Civil War* (London, 1983).

5. See pp. 44, 48.

6. See the descriptive analysis of these newsreels and their voice-over commentaries in A. Aldgate, *Cinema and History: British Newsreels and the Spanish Civil War* (London, 1979), esp. pp. 00.

7. Interview in BBC Wales' series 'The Collier's Crusade' (Episode 3), broadcast in 1979 and based on the work of H. Francis.

8. *Western Mail and South Wales News*, 7 November 1936. In the nature of things it is impossible to estimate how far Mr Thomas actually used (or even approved) the form of words adopted by the reporter.

General Hugh Sutton (1867–1928) was a hero of the Second South African and First World Wars, a guards officer who was mentioned in despatches more times than any other staff officer of his generation; See *Who was Who*, 1919–30.

9. 'Collier's Crusade' interview.

10. *Western Mail*, 25 August 1938 (Lady Bute's article) and 8 September 1938 (FHT's letter). Further to the question of air raids on civilian targets, see p. 00 and note 123.

11. See *Cardiff and the Spanish Civil War*, esp. pp. 114–16.

12. The latter pictures were printed in the *Daily Worker* on 12 November 1936; see C. Brothers, *War and Photography: A Cultural History* (London, 1997), p. 177. The shots had been retrieved from destruction by Arturo Barea, who realised their immense propaganda value, when the government censorship office was abandoned on 6 November. He later delivered them to the Communist Party offices in Madrid; A. Barea, *La Forja de un Rebelde: 3. La Llama* (Madrid, 1984), p. 213.

13. Evidence from Mrs Elin Williams, Newport, Dyfed.

14. Quoted in H. Francis, *Miners Against Fascism*, p. 160.

15. Mr Abse himself was discouraged from volunteering by the Welsh miners' leader, Arthur Horner; ibid., p. 172. An exception to his rule was Lance Rogers, of Merthyr, who was also nineteen years old at the time of his recruitment.

16. D. Abad de Santillan, *Porque perdimos la guerra* (Buenos Aires, 1940) pp. 174–5. (I owe this reference to my colleague, Dr Chris Ealham.)

17. The sinister atmosphere prevailing in Barcelona during these days was vividly described by George Orwell, who arrived in the Catalan capital on leave from the Aragon front only a few days before SH; see *Homage to Catalonia* (Penguin edn, Harmondsworth, 1989), esp. pp. 97–100.

18. R. Fraser, *Blood of Spain: An Oral History of the Spanish Civil War* (Harmondsworth, 1984), p. 377.

19. See p. 108.

20. Aznar, *Historia Militar II*, 197 (see below, n. 27).

21. Letter to me from Leo Abse, 4 March 1997.

22. D. Abse, *Ash on a Young Man's Sleeve* (1954), pp. 78–80.

23. See General Eoin O'Duffy to FHT, 1 September 1937 (original in FHT's possession), reproduced on page 122.

24. See R. Stradling, 'Orwell and the Spanish Civil War – A Historical Critique' in C. Norris (ed), *Inside the Myth – Orwell: Views from the Left* (London, 1984), pp. 103–25, for discussion of the reasons for this.

25. In the 1960s, researching his PhD thesis, Hywel Francis was given access to the text and interviewed FHT. But in the published volume only passing mention of the case is made; *Miners against Fascism*, pp. 175 and 178.

26. The original typescript ('Spanish *Legionario*: A Professional Soldier in Spain') and one carbon copy, remain in the author's possession. Though he wrote home on a regular basis, none of this correspondence has survived, and FHT retains very few other relics of his service in Spain.

27. The main works of military history which cover the period of FHT's active service in Spain (October 1936–May 1937) are (in order of publication): M. Aznar, *Historia Militar de la Guerra de España* (3 vols, 3rd edn, Madrid, 1958–63), vols I and II; J.M. Martínez Bande, *Frente de Madrid* (Barcelona, 1976) and idem., *La Marcha Sobre Madrid* (Madrid, 1982). The latter expert is more scholarly and less overtly pro-Nationalist than the former.

INTRODUCTION

Apart from the strictly military sections of Hugh Thomas' comprehensive study (*Spanish Civil War*), no equivalent work exists in English. See, however, the useful extended essay by R. Proctor, 'A Military History of the Spanish Civil War, 1936–1939' in J. Cortada (ed.), *Historical Dictionary of the Spanish Civil War* (Westport, Connecticut, 1982), pp. 515–31.

28. P. Kemp, *Mine Were of Trouble* (London, 1957). This is the only other published memoir of a British volunteer in Franco's army. It is possible that FHT's relevant faculties were sharpened by his acting as batman to the captain of his company for some six weeks, during which one of his duties was to attend councils of war. See p. 91.

29. The inside back cover contains a 'wallet' section into which the owner has inserted his NUS membership card, a receipt for his laboratory/workshop fees at the college and a scrap of paper bearing the stamp of the 'XV Brigada Internacional' with what seems to be an autograph of Harry Pollitt. Opposite this collection, SH has affixed a sewing needle to an advertisement page.

30. The diary was originally written in pencil. Over the years Elin Williams noticed that the script was fading badly, and (not without some agonizing in the cause of 'authenticity') eventually asked her daughter to overline it in ink.

31. The former has been acquired during research for various earlier publications, including *Cardiff and the Spanish Civil War* and *Crusades in Conflict: Ireland and the Spanish Civil War, 1936–39* (forthcoming, Manchester, 1998). Many of the latter are listed in the bibliographical section of *Crusades in Conflict*.

32. W. Gregory, *The Shallow Grave* (London, 1986). A few months after Brunete, the Irish Hispanophile Walter Starkie visited the area. 'It was a grim sight [he noted] as one walked across the battlefield to see the countless tiny hummocks of earth covering the hastily buried bodies.' 'Spanish War Diary', Trinity College, Dublin, Ms. 9193/1–293.

33. It may be presumed that the date of her son's death had been confirmed to Mrs Hamm by the comrade who brought the diary back from Spain. In conversation with me (3 September 1997) Lance Rogers clearly remembered Sid being shot down, on the first morning of the offensive, in the vicinity of Villanueva de la Cañada. However, in the Memorial Souvenir, *British Battalion, XV International Brigade* (London,

1939), issued by the International Brigade Association, SH is recorded as having died on 10 July.

34. A useful introduction in English is J.H. Galey, 'Bridegrooms of Death. A Profile Study of the Spanish Foreign Legion,' *Journal of Contemporary History* 4 (1969), pp. 47–64. See also, J.F. Gárate Córdoba et al, *La Legión Española: Cincuenta Años de Historia* (2 vols, Madrid, 1970–3), and F. Gómez de Travecedo, *La Legión Española* (Madrid, 1958).

35. S. Payne, *Politics and the Military in Modern Spain* (Stanford, California, 1967), passim.

36. The reader who wishes more information on the original regiments may consult R. Quatrefages, *Los Tercios* (Madrid, 1983), or G. Parker, *The Army of Flanders: The logistics of Spanish victory and defeat in the Low Countries' Wars, 1567–1659* (Cambridge, 1972).

37. A detailed account of this *escándalo* will be found in Thomas, *Spanish Civil War*, pp. 501–4. On Millán Astray, see the profile in Cortada, *Dictionary*, pp. 337–8.

38. For the army of Africa's campaign, I have relied mainly upon Martínez Bande, *La Marcha*, esp. p. 125ff.

39. Q. in F. Díaz-Plaja, *Anecdotario de la Guerra Civil Española* (Madrid, 1995), p. 67.

40. The so-called *'auxiliares indígenos'* of the Army of Africa in fact outnumbered the *Tercio* units by over two to one; see F. Gárate Córdoba, 'Los Moros en la Guerra de España,' *Historia y Vida* 23 (1990), pp. 88–99. For further comment on their role, see below, pp. 137–8, 143, 150, 152.

41. *El Adelanto de Salamanca* (main Nationalist newspaper of the north-central region) carried a prominent recruiting advertisement for the Legion during the autumn months of 1936. In the files of the Nationalist Foreign Office, various internal memos from this period refer to Franco's ruling that all overseas volunteers deemed to be suitable for service should be enrolled in the *Tercio*; Madrid, Archivo del Ministerio de Asuntos Exteriores, Archivo de Burgos, Legajo R1059.

42. See p. 82.

43. J.M. Martínez Bande, *La Batalla del Ebro* (Madrid, 1988), pp. 135–50. The VI *Bandera* held the notorious Hill 481 for ten days against repeated attacks by all three English-speaking battalions. As in the case of their earlier encounter on the Jarama, the decision went in favour of the defence.

44. Cortada, *Dictionary*, pp. 211–12.

45. The best general study is Bill Alexander, *British Volunteers for Liberty: Spain, 1936–39* (London, 1982). An extremely effective personal account of the Battalion has recently appeared, based upon the author's extensive contemporary diaries; F. Thomas, *Tilting at Windmills: A Memoir of the Spanish Civil War* (East Lansing, Michigan, 1996). This veteran arrived in Spain shortly after SH, and served for eighteen consecutive months until demobilization in late 1938.

46. Alexander, *British Volunteers*, p. 130.

47. See 'Spain Welcomes the Brigadistas', *The Volunteer – Journal of the Veterans of the Abraham Lincoln Brigade*, XIX, i (winter 1996–7). However, the offer of Spanish citizenship turned out to be more than the Spanish Constitution could stand and, in the end, it was made conditional upon renunciation of the veterans' existing statehood. I know of no one who was prepared to accept this condition.

SPANISH *LEGIONARIO*: A PROFESSIONAL SOLDIER IN SPAIN

by F.H. *THOMAS*

CONTENTS

PROLOGUE

THE CREDO OF THE LEGION

The spirit of the Legion is unique and without equal; of a blind ferociousness in combat; to shorten the distance with the enemy and to charge him with the bayonet.

The spirit of comradeship is such that under no circumstances must a wounded or dead *Legionario* be abandoned on the battlefield, even if it means the death of all.

The spirit of campaigning is never to fall out on a march; the *Legionario* never succumbs to fatigue nor pain, hunger nor thirst nor sleep; he must accomplish all orders given him, without question.

The *Legionario* must obey until death. He must always, always fight without rest, without counting the days, the months, the years. Death in combat is the highest honour; comes only once, comes without pain.

The *Legionario* and the Legion must run towards the sound of firing, by day, by night, always, always, with order or without.

'The Legion to me' is a cry the *Legionario* must answer by his presence, with or without reason.

The flag of the Legion is the most glorious of all flags because it is stained with the blood of all its Legionarios.

Long Live Spain!

Long Live the Legion!

Illustrations of these are contained in the Legion history which follows the credo in the small booklet, issued to each recruit to be learned from cover to cover. Of these, the following will be sufficient to illustrate how well they have been carried out:

Once a whole section – some fifty men – gave their lives recovering the body of a dead comrade; in one terrible march in Morocco four *Legionarios* – one a German – dropped dead on the march, but there were no stragglers. Holding out to the last in a Moroccan blockhouse to enable their comrades to retreat, fifteen volunteers gave their lives in the 'Blockhouse of Death'.[1]

CHAPTER ONE.

Metamorphosis.

"Why" is a wonderful word. Its corollary is naturally "seek and ye shall find", and it is through these that I managed to turn aside that veil of respectable slavery of which the ideal is a safe job and a white collar.

Leaving a good secondary school the open-air life of a poultry farmer seemed attractive for a few years until despairing of the "cash in hand" ever catching up the "cash paid out" column, I became the accepted idea of a commercial traveller complete with sample bag (full), order-book (empty), and salesmanship. My goods were mainly tinned stuff but without sardines, for which I was afterwards thankful when eating nauseating quantities of them as "iron-rations", as to have the stain of them on my "sales-consciousness" would have been the last straw.

Two-and-a-half years of this was two years too long, as, my calls on each customer being monthly, after the initial period of becoming friendly with them, my mental outlook became again stationary and I began to crave for fresh fields to conquer. Business was not to be thought of again as the main topics seemed to be confined to "business is bad" and "how's the weather", both depressingly morbid topics.

As a welcome relief the "Spanish" War "broke". Here would now be the place for disclaiming heroics about how touched I was by the sacredness of General Franco's cause but conscience compels me to say it only seemed to me the opportunity to enquire into a professional soldier's life.

The more I thought of it, the better idea it seemed and so October 6,1936, saw me aboard the Booth liner "Hilary" bound from Liverpool to Lisbon having unearthed my passport, the relic of a previous holiday. The die was cast, and on General Franco's behalf

The first page of the text of FHT's memoirs in the original 1937 typescript.

CHAPTER ONE

METAMORPHOSIS

'Why' is a wonderful word. Its corollary is naturally 'seek and ye shall find', and it is through these that I managed to turn aside that veil of respectable slavery of which the ideal is a safe job and a white collar.

After leaving a good secondary school, the open-air life of a poultry farmer seemed attractive for a few years. Until, despairing of the 'cash in hand' ever catching up the 'cash paid out' column, I became the accepted idea of a commercial traveller, complete with sample bag (full), order book (empty), and salesmanship. My goods were mainly tinned stuff but without sardines, for which I was afterwards thankful when eating nauseating quantities of them as 'iron rations', as to have the stain of them on my 'sales consciousness' would have been the last straw.[2] Two and a half years of this was two years too long; calls on each customer being monthly, after the initial period of becoming friendly with them, my mental outlook became again stationary, and I began to crave for fresh fields to conquer. A different line of business was not to be thought of, as the main topics of conversation seemed to be confined to 'business is bad' and 'How's the weather?' – both depressingly morbid topics.

As a welcome relief the Spanish War 'broke out'. This point would be the expected one for proclaiming heroics about how touched I was by the sacredness of General Franco's cause; but conscience compels me to say that it seemed to me the opportunity to enquire into a professional soldier's life. The more I thought of it, the better idea it seemed. And so 6 October 1936 saw me aboard the Booth liner *Hilary*, bound from Liverpool to Lisbon, having first unearthed my passport, the relic of a previous holiday. The die was cast, and on General Franco's behalf – by virtue of his possessing a picturesque Foreign Legion. Besides, I do not like Communism – a viewpoint afterwards confirmed a hundred times over.

The days on the water passed, enlivened by the yarns of a professional big-game hunter, a German, on his way to the Amazon once more. A day late, owing to heavy seas preventing our entrance to the harbour, we reached Leixoes, the dock area of Oporto. Here, hunter Hans and I went ashore and spent an all too short day seeing the sights and sampling the port. Regaining the harbour, everything seemed to be lurching, even the ship, while the gangway would keep coming up to and going away from our feet. So we left Leixoes with confused recollections of picturesque whitewashed or mosaic tiled houses going up to the hills in terraces; a weather-worn church towering in its medieval age above these modern upstarts, with the path leading up to the growling lion's head carved on its front formed from huge blocks of stone intersected by grass; and an awe-ful respect for its famous wine.

The next day we reached Lisbon where, if the calendar had not informed us that the day following, being the eleventh of October, was a Sunday, one would never have known, as all the shops, cafes, fish and vegetable markets were wide open. Lisbon is a queer place, built on hills, and some of the streets are very steep – although they do not seem to present much difficulty to the dirty, old-fashioned trams which (with bulb-horns blaring away) continuously compete with the all-powerful motor car horns in one dreadful deafening din.[3] The churches, as usual in Catholic countries, are fine places, while the Portuguese government buildings seem opulent for such a small Republic. Having sufficient British money still on me, I was pleasantly surprised by its spending power.

Bidding goodbye to Hans, who was sailing that afternoon to Manaos in Brazil, I went for the night to a nice little hotel near the fine Rocio, main square of Lisbon, calling on the way at a little bar where I met a typical British remittance man, boozy and brainless.[4] Yet it takes all sorts to make the world. The next morning, after bacon and eggs – spoilt by frying in olive oil – after much trouble I found the insurgents' Lisbon office, in the Rua Castelho, where I got my passport visa-ed to enter Spain at Badajoz.[5] Finding the train did not leave until after midnight, a hurried visit to the small Zoological Gardens proved rewarding, as having to get there meant walking up the beautiful Avenida da Liberdade. This is a magnificently wide, palm-lined avenue, divided in the centre by an artificial rill running down over moss-grown miniature waterfalls, the whole overlooked by a large obelisk erected to commemorate the overthrow of Spanish overlordship over three hundred years ago.[6] A short journey to see part of the British-built Portuguese Navy rounded off the evening and, boarding the train, I was soon *en route* for Badajoz.

The train arrived at Elvas, the last Portuguese station, about eight o'clock the next morning and after a cursory customs examination we proceeded to Badajoz, first station over the border.

CHAPTER TWO

ON TOUR

Lisbon is a cosmopolitan city and many people can manage some English, so I had not been afflicted by the curse of Babel. Things were different as soon as I alighted on the platform of remote Badajoz, where my ignorance of the local tongue was brought cruelly home. However, with the aid of a midget dictionary purchased at home in one of the famous threepenny and sixpenny stores,[7] I managed to convey the idea that I was neither an anarchist nor a spy but only a volunteer, mad perhaps, but in a politically acceptable sort of way.

Given the freedom of the platform while the customs clerk got in touch with the local military big-wig, I chummed up with a jolly, fat customs policeman. Just coming off duty, he volunteered, once my permission to remain in Spain had come through, to take me into Badajoz, to get a military safe-conduct. During the two-mile walk downhill into the town we became quite friendly on the strength of the magic dictionary. Approaching the massive walls of the town I tried to recall the story of their storming during the Peninsular War – with signal unsuccess![8]

ON TOUR

Getting my pass, I found I should have to wait twenty-four hours for a train to Burgos – Provisional Government HQ – and so set out to see the sights. As they seemed to consist of only small *vino* (wine) bars, I soon had to get my last two pounds changed. My friend again came to the rescue, wrangling with the changer as if it were his own money. Comparing values later with other foreigners I found I had good value for my money. Towards evening, since he was going on duty at the station again, he left me in the charge of a one-eyed friend of his, a *vino* bar proprietor. I had no place to go for the night, and this new benefactor took me to a nice little *posada* where I got a bedroom. Up early next morning I found there was nothing to pay except a tip to the maidservant. As a foreigner who was going to fight for Spain, I was welcome to a night's lodging and breakfast, while the maidservant gave me a holy medal – I still have it – to bring me luck.

At the station I again met my policeman friend, who got me my ticket and wished me 'God Speed'. Trying to thank him for his kindness I pointed out a phrase in my dictionary which meant 'I am very grateful to you' but, my finger slipped in turning the book towards him, and instead I pointed to 'I am very sorry'! However, I saw the mistake in time to rectify it. This is merely one illustration of the difficulties under which I laboured for months before picking up sufficient Spanish to get along. My sixpenny dictionary was of invaluable help in the beginning, but within a few days of the above incident I lost it, and thenceforth trusted to my luck and good judgement and other people's patience. For instance, one day, just after joining my company, I drew a burst from a machine-gun on myself and my luckless comrades by incautiously exposing myself to fire. My corporal immediately exclaimed *'mal alegre'* or 'bad luck', referring to my foolhardy courage.[9] I thought he was complimenting me on my good luck and for some months after used the phrase to wish my long-suffering comrades 'good luck'. Again, it took me time to get the right pronunciation of *'carreta'*, *'cartera'* and *'carretera'* (meaning gas-mask, wallet and road, respectively) and often used to ask for my 'road' instead of my 'gas-mask'.

Once the train pulled out of Badajoz, I settled down in my empty compartment to read a week-old English newspaper purchased at Lisbon. Chugging along at about thirty miles per hour – the tracks are so badly laid that they would break up if the engine did more – the train headed northwards. It climbed higher and higher through and above more desolate regions of rock-carved canyons, in the bottom of which mountain streams ran, with here and there a patch of cultivated ground or an olive grove to show that people did, indeed, inhabit a small part of the wilderness.[10]

Northwards, past the mighty Sierra de Gredos, was Salamanca, where we arrived at dusk. After a long wait, which everybody improved by sleeping, we went on through the night, still calling at every shanty along the line as we had done ever since leaving Badajoz. A night's journey through Portugal in a third-class coach, Iberian variety – wooden seats, the partition between the compartments only continued to halfway, no heating – had convinced me of British superiority in this mode of transport. My discomfiture was keener still on the long haul through Castile, where the climb from the Tagus valley to the high northern *meseta* also, for the first time, made me aware of the facts that summer was over and I only had my thin summer clothes.

Early next morning, the rising sun awoke my fellow passengers and I, and to a man the former rose to open their food baskets. Every Spaniard, in this class at least, carries one if his journey is of any length, owing to the difficulty of getting any food on route. Several proffered breakfasts, reminding me that it was twenty-four hours since I had eaten, and I gladly accepted cold meat, cheese and bread, washing it down with copious amounts of *vino*.[11] About nine a.m., after having passed through a more fully settled countryside for several hours, we arrived at Burgos. Birthplace of the Cid, Burgos was then the seat of the Junta, or Provisional Government of the insurgents, led by the aged General Cabanellas. A benevolent-looking old liberal, his day came and went; just as the liberals on the other side were displaced, so was he as the extreme forces on either side gained power. Today, crushed by obscurity, he lives a life of retirement like that of Wales' Grand Old Liberal only appearing at the Spanish equivalents of the *Eisteddfodau*.[12]

After leaving the station, crossing the river, trudging up a shady and picturesque promenade, through streets of the Middle Ages, I found the *Cuartel*, headquarters of the Divisional-General of the district. Here the usual hand-signs, dictionary, etc., and the magic password *'Inglés'* – licence for most madcap doings in Spain – produced no more than a view through a partly opened door of the Big Noise in Person, from whose orderly I presently received instructions to report at some other barracks on the other side of the river.[13]

A move in this direction took me past the Hotel Norte y Londres, where I had been told British journalists were staying, and past the magnificent old cathedral, one of the finest in Spain. At the barracks I was initially prevented from entering by two sentries with fixed bayonets until the corporal of the guard appeared. He handed me over to a military clerk who, taking my height and weight, asked me to 'call back after three, as the doctor likes his siesta'. Thus, though anxiously waiting to join such an energetic army, I was forced to cool my heels. So off I wandered to eat some bread and cheese (purchased by the crude device of pointing), to make an attempt to flirt with a young and pretty barmaid, and to see something of the city. Business as usual seemed to be the motto of Burgos and, except for the recruiting notices and the multicoloured uniforms to be seen everywhere, it was difficult to realise there was a war on at all.

When I returned at last to the barracks, the doctor, a cheerful young lieutenant, ordered me to take off my shirt, pounded me in the chest and back, smiled at me and gave me a slip of signed paper marked *'útil'* (fit), telling me to return to the *Cuartel*. Here a young, half-English artillery officer told me in English that to complete my enlistment in the Legion I should have to go back down the line to Valladolid, as all the soldiers and barracks in Burgos belonged to the Regular Army. While speaking to him, I could not help remarking how slack the discipline there appeared to be, as privates were continually interrupting him to ask who I was and what I was doing there. He assured me I should have a different tale to tell of the Legion discipline, explaining that in the Regular Army, being conscripted, Pedro considers himself as good as his master, since the officers themselves are conscripts.

At last an orderly brought me a safe-conduct and a railway voucher – the first I had received – and told me to proceed to Valladolid. The young officer having by now gone about his business, I had to trust that Providence would direct me when I got there. The orderly also emphasised that the train left in half an hour, so, dashing out of the place, I commandeered a young urchin to guide me quickly to the station. After this scurried start, I arrived in time at the station; indeed, in the event I proved to have arrived two or three hours before the train left. Organization of the Spanish variety, that's what it was![14]

CHAPTER THREE

EL TERCIO

In the middle of the night the train arrived at Valladolid. Left stranded on the platform, I approached a group of Fascists (recognizable by their dark-blue shirts) who, realising the difficulty I was in, kindly took me to their local headquarters in an empty mansion.[15] Knocking at the door for some time produced an inspection through a small grille window, and then admission. The sentry, explaining that he had been asleep, took us upstairs to the dormitory. The sleeping Fascists awoke and plied me with food, questions and a blanket. A short sleep, shortened further by watching a friendly all-in wrestling match brought the daylight, coffee and bread.

A guide was deputed to take me to the barracks. Here I was subjected again to the chest punching and, after a short wait, shown with two Spanish volunteers into another room. There was a huge map on the wall bespattered with pins, on which several officers were working. One of these took us in hand and soon got our

The division of Spain, autumn 1936.

La Coruña

Santander
Guernica
FRANCE
Seté

Oviedo
Bilbao

PYRENEES

Pamplona

Burgos

Huesca

R. Ebro

Valladolid
Zaragoza

Salamanca
Barcelona

Leixoes

SIERRA DE GUADARRAMA

Avila
Guadalajara

SIERRA DE GREDOS
Madrid

PORTUGAL
Teruel

Talavera
de la Reina
Toledo

R. Tagus
Chinchón

Cáceres
Aranjuez

Valencia
de Alcántara
Madrigueras
Valencia

Lisbon
Elvas
Badajoz
Albacete

Alicante

Córdoba

Seville
Cartagena

Granada

Cadiz
Málaga
Almería

Gibraltar

Tetuan

SPANISH MOROCCO
Melilla

Republican-held territory
Nationalist-held territory

papers filled in, in my case with the aid of French. Our fingerprints, being impressed upon the papers, clinched the deal, and I had become a second-class legionary, engaged for the duration of the campaign. It was ten days since I had left Liverpool.

The Spanish Foreign Legion (as it is called in English) is not really one Legion but, pre-1937, two, and since this spring three Legions. It is known as *El Tercio*, and its three component parts as the *Primera*, *Segunda* and *Tercera Legiones del Tercio*, enlistment being voluntary and lasting for one, three, five or ten year periods – with, at present, the war's duration also. Formed originally in the Middle Ages from foreigners for overseas service, it received many recruits from the British Isles during the religious troubles, especially the Irish supporters of the O'Neills and O'Donnells.[16] Being disbanded on the collapse of the Spanish Empire, it was not re-formed until 1920, when the Moroccan defences were being reorganized. Its badge – reminiscent of its ancient foundations – was a battleaxe, crossed by a musket and a crossbow. The French Foreign Legion having proved so successful against the Moors, a Spanish attempt to create a similar voluntary army was initiated. The rates of pay are far better than those of its better-known counterpart, but it has never been so popular with foreigners, a public outcry against the scandalously severe disciplinary requirements (in 1921) having a lot to do with it.

Each of the two pre-1936 Legions consisted of four *banderas* or regiments of infantry, each of four *compañías*, while there was also an *escuadrón* of cavalry, in all some six or seven thousand men, eighty per cent of whom were Spanish or Portuguese. An unsympathetic Republican government disbanded the Seventh and Eighth *Banderas* and the cavalry in 1932, but the outbreak of the 'movement' in 1936 saw their restoration.[17] Many other *banderas* have been formed since, but with their long and successful record in the Moorish War, these original eight are still the criterion. Another result of the large increase was the transfer of personnel from the residual six to create a nuclei of veterans for the newer *banderas*. This deficit has never been made up because of the enormous losses of the Legion in the war.[18] As, apart from the Moors, they form the only shock-troops of Franco's army, they have to bear the brunt of heavy offence and defence. The Regular Army is composed of conscripts – 'one volunteer is worth three Spanish conscripts' – noted more for their running than their staying powers. These regulars are usually used for 'mopping up', as are the Fascist battalions. The Carlist Army, on the other hand, has been very much to the front, especially in the North, and also as holding-troops on the Marañosa front south of Madrid.[19]

My greatest compatriot, Mr Lloyd George, has seen fit to sympathize with the Basque province of Biscay in its 'fight for freedom' but a study of the Carlist Army would tell a different story. All volunteers, in the main it is composed of Basques from the provinces of Navarre, Alava and Guipúzcoa – two-thirds of the entire Basque country; Basques, moreover, actuated not by petty nationalism but by a greater motive, that of Nationalist Spain. When the movement broke out they formed a precarious island in the midst of a Red Sea, holding on grimly while a causeway was slowly built towards them from Seville in the far south, from the provinces of Estremadura and Old Castile. Which is the greater, a living ideal of a united peninsula or the nationalism of a petty province not representative of Basque aspirations?[20]

I should mention here that a second-class *Legionario* (or private) draws in all six pesetas and ten centimos a day, of which he actually receives three pesetas in his hand, one peseta ten cents daily being saved against the time of his discharge (when his debit amount for clothes has to be cleared off), and two pesetas being deducted daily for his food. In the firing line, he gets eighty-five centimos extra a day thus making the net daily pay for which he risks his life actually 3.85 pesetas (one shilling and fourpence). Owing to the low standard of living in Spain and Morocco – ten shillings weekly being a fair artisan's wages – there are always recruits as, when free billets are taken into account, men are actually better off in the force. The Legionary's conscript brother, however, is worse off, only receiving one penny daily during training, doubled on active service. The latter is also unpaid when in hospital, recovering the back pay on return to his regiment; the *Legionario's* five-daily pay is maintained when under treatment, another little privilege for, after all, one dare not mortify one's right hand.

To return to my recruiting officer at Valladolid, from whom I have far digressed; I and the two other recruits – or *quintos* as they are known from their fancied resemblance to fifth-class soldiers – were given five pesetas (day's pay plus day's food allowance), put in the charge of three Civil Guards and entrained for Talavera de la Reina, temporary headquarters of the Second Legion.[21] The journey was unremarkable, except for the length of time it took (one and a half days) and for the small crowds which gathered at stations en route to hear an 'Englishman' – for they know not Wales – singing 'Men of Harlech', and 'Tipperary', and imploring them to 'Kiss Me My Sweet'.

CHAPTER FOUR

TRAINING DAYS AND TRAINING WAYS

A van, aptly resembling a hearse, was waiting for us at Talavera station. Along with our guards (still with us as a protection against our playing the confidence trick on the recruiting officer) we were whisked off to the training barracks. There, being British, I was looked upon as being some sort of strange animal by the other *quintos*, probably being the first one the majority had ever seen. One of them, however, speaking English a little, immediately put me at ease while awaiting the officer in charge. The officer, a *teniente* (lieutenant) soon appeared and got down to interrogating us three recruits. Speaking perfect English, *Teniente* Méndez was one of the best Spanish types, a fair and just gentleman – except for the usual streak of ferocity accentuated by years of Legion life, which burst out occasionally, especially when idiotic mistakes were made at drill. Explaining to me the rigours of Legion active service, he gave me the option of making up my mind as to my suitability in one or two days, offering me my discharge by issuing me with discharge papers as 'unfit for training' if I decided to accept them. He told me frankly – not knowing that I am naturally pale-faced – that he thought that I would speedily collapse in the trenches. This unusual offer will illustrate his nature while it cannot suggest to the reader his military qualities; seconded for active service, he gave his life before that Christmas in the operations around Madrid.

It being a Sunday [18 October] there were no drills, so after my first Legion dinner, the English-speaking Spaniard, Guillermo Ramírez, and I went around Talavera, during which I learnt of his father, an artillery officer, killed with the other officers, both infantry and artillery, by their own men at the Madrid military camp of Carabanchel on the outbreak of hostilities.[22] Having received light-green breeches, a shirt, a vest, boots, *capote* – a thick khaki cloak, buttoned up on three sides, and easily convertible into a ten-foot blanket – and rifle, next morning saw us out on the rifle range for firing and bomb-throwing practice. In the afternoon came drill.

The Spanish Legion must be one of the few military forces where men are drilled by use of whips. Drastic and medieval, like so much of Spain, but often necessary with some of the brutal animals which are attracted to their peacetime ranks. Few, even of those so punished, complain of it, for in this country – where many have no more learning than to be able to read and write, where many cannot even do this, and where those who have been to secondary education are called 'students' as if they were university men – might is right. Lack of knowledge and other similar deficiencies account for the division in the present struggle among the actual people themselves (not the intelligentsia) into the extreme elements of left- and right-wing parties.

During training, the whip is applied to all parts of the body – some of its exponents being particularly adept at picking out their spot – by anybody from the rank of corporal upwards, even for the most trivial offences on the drill ground; but owing to the possibilities of retaliation is rarely used on the front line.[23] When I mention that discipline is carried to such fantastic lengths as to insist upon a lower rank, when speaking to a higher rank, putting his hand up to the salute and keeping it there until told to take it down; that to approach an officer in his room with a request, message or order means – in the correct sequence – taking one's cap off, asking permission to enter the room, coming to attention a metre distant, a statement of being at his disposal, giving the message, receiving his answer, asking if he has any further commands, a step backwards, a repetition of being at his disposal, an about turn, replacing the cap outside the room before an NCO grabs the luckless culprit for being improperly dressed. Or again, that an officer entering a dug-out or place in which soldiers are, requires all from sergeant downwards to stand up and take off their caps; that for a man to leave a marching column for natural reasons requires that man to salute while asking the corporal for permission and keep at the salute while the latter gets the sergeant's permission for him; then will my readers realise the archaic principles which guide the *Legionario*.[24]

As a foreigner I was exempt from the whip – all foreigners except the Portuguese are.[25] Furthermore, *Teniente* Méndez took a French recruit, Pierre—— and myself apart for drill, coaching us patiently in the half-understood Spanish drill.[26] The other recruits, including Frantisek Shostek, a Czech who could speak Spanish, were drilled apart under the direction of a black Cuban sergeant named La Franca and several long-service corporals. Needless to say the whips were kept flashing here for such offences as turning right instead of left. In return for this suffering, the volunteer is given the right to be called *'caballero Legionario'* or 'gentleman legionary'. It can be amusing to watch an uncouth peasant, for the nonce a gentleman, insisting upon being called such by an incautious bar-tender.[27]

Next day after dinner, having had the firing practice again in the morning, all the recruits, some forty in number, were fallen in. Two parties from the Fifth and Sixth *Banderas* had arrived for recruits so we were divided into two lots, one for each *bandera*. The Czech, Frenchman and myself were allotted to the Sixth *Bandera*. In charge of the corporal and two lance-corporals from this *bandera* we set out in motor omnibuses. Bound for the front after one day and a half of instruction – quite a record, even for the Legion! However, recruits at this time were few in number – only seven had entered the *Banderín de Enganche* (recruiting depot) the previous week – while for myself I was glad that no time was to be wasted. At home I had not even thought of the possibility of being held up through lack of training.[28]

One thing I did regret. This was the inability to see more of two fellow Britishers met the previous evening. They were two young sailors – a Canadian and an Englishman – from HMS *Barham* at Gibraltar, who had swum ashore to Spanish territory to join the Legion and see the hostilities. They were then in Talavera with the Seventh *Bandera*, still doing instructions when I left. Just before I got to Talavera they had had a terrible beating with the whips, having been suspected by a drunken sergeant of poisoning wells. An apology to them followed next day but they still bore the marks of the whip when I saw them, and had determined to clear out as soon as possible.[29]

CHAPTER FIVE
UNDER FIRE

That same evening, the omnibus pulled up with a jerk in the shell-torn market square of the small village of Casa Rubios del Monte. On the way we had been passing wrecked villages so that to be landed in the middle of one was not much of a surprise. It had in fact only been taken from the enemy two days previously.[30] We were immediately taken to the *Plana Mayor* – or *Bandera* HQ – where a staff officer allotted us to one or other of the four companies in the *Bandera*. Frantisek Shostek and myself went to the Twenty-Fourth Company while Pierre – who was to be killed in action the following February during the operations against the Valencia road –

went to the Twenty-First.[31] The rest of the recruits being Spaniards, with one or two Portuguese, did not interest us much.

All of us (however) were kept for the night at the *Plana* where Frantisek and I met another foreigner, a Hungarian named Georges Kozma. As an illustration of the types of foreigner found in the actual Legion – and not those who are in the Italian 'Black Arrows' or German Mechanized groups – the following might be of interest.[32]

Kozma, a tall young man of twenty-three, wore the typical small, pointed beard of his race and had come to Spain to fight for his (RC) religion. He had been educated at the universities of Budapest, Rome and Louvain, graduating out of the latter as a member of the Catholic Missionary Society of the White Fathers. Before coming to Spain he had had some experience of missionary work in Algeria, and thus, besides the Hungarian, German, Italian and French which he knew perfectly, he had smatterings of Arabic and Spanish. A little English rounded off his linguistic accomplishments. He was one type – the philosophical religious crusader.[33]

In contrast, Frantisek Shostek, only eighteen, had robbed his father's safe and bolted to Genoa in Italy with the proceeds. There, in bad company, he had soon been robbed of his money and collected the germs of future venereal disease. Stranded, without anything, he had gone to the Legion recruiting office in Genoa and had been shipped from there via Seville to Talavera. Here was another type – impecunious, a criminal without hope, taking to the Legion for shelter and obscurity.

With the third type, the adventurer, and the fourth, Fascist, type, one has the main divisions among the foreigners.[34] The Spanish volunteers were the same, with the addition of the patriotic type, and also those who had joined to get protection for their families from the Fascists, or simply in order to be on what they considered the winning side.

Frantisek and I learned from Kozma, through the medium of French, a short summary of the present position. He also related a story, confirmed by others present, concerning a Portuguese – a mounted dispatch rider of the *bandera* – who, only a few days earlier, had ridden by mistake into Casa Rubios, when held by the Reds. To appreciate how easy it was to make this sort of mistake it must be understood that until the following December the fighting resembled guerrilla warfare, the Nationalists seldom occupying trenches as, our advance being so swift at this stage, there existed no time in which to construct them. A village being usually the objective to be attained in a day's fighting, the bulk of the *bandera* would sleep in the abandoned houses, one company usually lying further out, in shallow pits sufficient to cover one's body, as an advance guard. As our flanks were usually exposed to open country there were often villages to our rear which had seen neither our troops or the enemy's. Thus, reaching the market square without noticing anything amiss, the Portuguese was captured before he could escape. A companion riding behind him got away but the unfortunate prisoner was beaten to death with rifle butts and sticks, his mutilated and jelly-like body being still on the square when our troops forced an entry a little later. This was a sample of the treatment that all foreign *Legionarios*, and Moors, got at this time if captured. However only one other foreigner was ever captured from my *bandera* during my time, of whom more later.[35]

Next morning, 21 October, we were up at six, and got our usual cup of black coffee. This time, however, they also issued a rasher of raw fatty bacon, a half kilo of bread, and a sausage. Being hungry, and without thinking, I ate the bread and bacon. I threw the sausage away – the Spanish variety being as hard as a board with slivers of bone enclosed with the meat in a tough skin container. I later discovered that I had blithely disposed of my whole day's 'iron rations'. There are only two meals in the Legion, lunch at midday and dinner in the evening; on rising, there is only coffee. One must save bread from the previous day if food is required with it.[36]

After this tragi-comic episode, Frantisek being without rifle or cartridge belt, and I without the latter, we were attached to the mule column of our company until our captain had time to allot us to definitive places. At seven a.m. the advance of our *bandera* and a

Moorish regiment started. Without opposition, several miles of ground were covered, but at last rifle bullets began whistling overhead for, although the mules were at least a quarter of a mile behind the troops, the enemy's militiamen were putrid shots. They used their rifles on the principle that the higher the sighting-block so the hitting power of the bullet increased, and consequently their bullets went high over the target aimed at! Thus the casualties of the *bandera* (with its 500–600 men) were only two killed and six wounded during the whole day's operation.

In the afternoon, the heavily wired, well-constructed trenches placed on the outskirts of Navalcarnero (our objective, on the main Madrid road to Portugal) came into view, facing us half a mile across the other side of a small valley. The enemy, seeing our troops advancing down the opposite slope with fixed bayonets, remembered previous appointments in Madrid, and were out of the trench and away. We crossed the trench and entered the village, where the church bell had only just stopped ringing its warning evacuation tocsin [alarm bell]. During the daylight which remained, a line of shallow pits was hastily dug between Navalcarnero and Madrid, occupied, and our advance halted. Eighteen kilometres of ground, a large village of strategic value, a plentiful supply of arms and munitions, and a few prisoners – who, according to an old Spanish custom, were immediately shot – had been gained at little cost. Our artillery had been conspicuous in this action by its near absence, as the Artillery Corps had, nearly to a man, gone over to the enemy side at the beginning of the war. Our victory had as usual been due to superior and controlled fire – both of rifles and machine-guns.

My own recollections of my first experience of action had been the sight of a dead man (the first I had seen) lying in a wood we had passed through; clothed as a peasant, apart from his cartridge belt and smashed rifle; a dry stream bed exposed to view from Navalcarnero where 'bees' [i.e., bullets] kept humming around us; and the anticlimax that night, after a hot meal of haricot beans and coffee, of sleeping beside the mules with mule-packs as a pillow, a miscellaneous collection of saddle blankets and *capotes* as blankets, with a snoring Frantisek and a garlic-smelling muleteer as bedfellows.

The next day I was equipped with a captured cartridge belt and sent to join my *escuadra* and its *cabo* (corporal), Luis López. I was in the First Squadron, First Platoon of the Second Section. (A company is divided into three sections, each under the command of an officer; a *sección* is made up of two *pelotóns*, each under a sergeant; a *pelotón* of three *escuadras* of seven men or under, with one corporal each.) My *cabo*, a big bluff Aragonese, was a kindly fellow who took great pride in turning the lone *'Inglés'* into an ideal *Legionario*, swinging a lot of the rougher, humdrum work on to the four unfortunate Spaniards who, with myself, made up his squad. They, however, did not object, on the contrary readily assisting me to learn their language, and often preventing others' attempts to take advantage of my ignorance. My sergeant, Angel Rodríguez, and *Alférez* (second-lieutenant), Don Leonardo Blanco, also gave me their assistance.

My introduction to my corporal found him with other NCOs and privates busily engaged at the ever-popular card gambling games of *'seis y media'* and *'monte'* in the rifle pits outside the town.[37] Card playing is the *Legionarios'* hobby, being indulged in during the delays in advances – in fact at all possible (and some impossible) times, even marathon games being indulged in occasionally. One of the latter commenced one evening in billets at Navalcarnero. Its participants, all corporals, played through the night and the next day, only ceasing when all the money present had been transferred from the losing many to the winning few. This was not at *'monte'* but *'seis y media'*, a game in which, given good players, the money will flow backwards and forwards for great lengths of time. Money and other valuables to the value of sixty or seventy pounds sterling was on the boards at this time, the *Legionarios* having had rich pickings since the previous July.

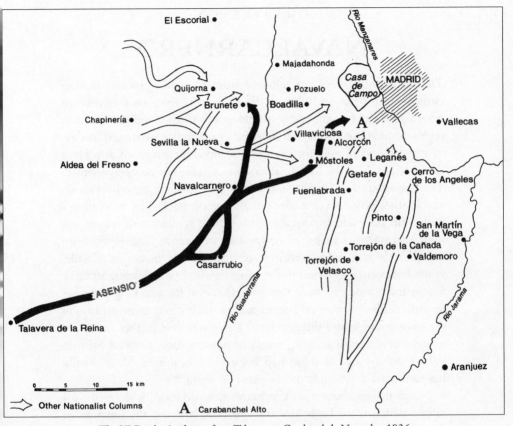

The VI Bandera's advance from Talavera to Carabanchel, November 1936.

CHAPTER SIX

NAVALCARNERO

That afternoon we were relieved from the rifle pits by another company, and put in billets in the village to give us a chance of exercising a right confined rigorously to the Legion and the Moorish regiments. Of this law, it will be sufficient to call it permitted looting of unoccupied houses for the first twenty-four hours of any place taken, after which we have to refrain or, at least, not be open about it. The regular troops, Fascists, and others are, however, prohibited from any looting whatsoever under penalty of death. I contented myself with a tin plate and spoon, also a nice thick blanket as my *capote* was none too warm at night, given my lack of a tunic. The nights from October throughout the winter are bitterly cold in central Castile, white frost being common in the mornings and often leading to thick fogs, which, foolishly, were never made use of for attacking purposes by either side.[38] However, I soon took a thick khaki tunic off one of the enemy and solved this problem. There was little further aid to my contentment, being nothing much of note in such a typical Spanish village. In any case if there had been, the ubiquitous Moor would have annexed it, probably on the previous night.[39]

Navalcarnero, thirty-two kilometres from Madrid, is the principal village between the latter city and Talavera. It is also the junction of the El Escorial road and was thus of strategic value.[40] Today, [1937] the main line of communications runs through it to the University City, and its possession is a guarantee against a flank attack from the Guadarrama mountains.[41] Many of the inhabitants had fled – evidently those with tender consciences – but many remained to carry on business as usual and the taverns were soon doing a roaring trade with wine, probably looted. At this stage, many inhabitants remained behind in their villages, only those of Socialist, Communist or Anarchist sympathies going with the retreating enemy, but later the latter put into force a system of compulsory evacuation, to conserve their manpower and to prevent sympathizers helping us as soldiers or farmers. We soon grew used to entering entirely deserted villages with perhaps only the village dogs to greet us.[42]

As this was civil war, Navalcarnero was no exception to other war zone villages, in that while the Reds were in occupation the houses of the wealthy and other so-called, or suspected, 'Fascists' were looted – grudges irrespective of political ones being also worked off. It seemed logical that, upon our entry, those houses unlooted but deserted were looked upon by us as 'Communist' houses, so that by the time the tide of war had rolled on only strictly neutral houses were left intact. One also got to be an expert in going straight to a plentiful supply of loot – just look for the poorer quarters of the town, as the wealthy had naturally been plundered by those in want. It became usual to find a house, the previous occupant of which had been a workman earning probably less than ten shillings per week, equipped with massive furniture and the choicest of bedding materials. It was some consolation to know later, when the winter really set in, that the walnut or mahogany furniture we were using as fuel had probably been 'scrounged' so many times that even Scotland Yard could not have found its indignant – or dead – legal owner.

Life passed pleasantly in Navalcarnero, turns of restful promenading and gambling in the village being interspersed with turns of duty in the rifle pits. In the latter, sentry duty passed pleasantly, with the sun overhead and the lovely view of the high and permanently snow-capped Guadarrama mountains forty or fifty kilometres to the north – the only sign of the war being our three pursuit aeroplanes which occasionally flew overhead going to reconnoitre Madrid. At night, with the crisp cold air and the beautiful moonlight playing tricks with shadows away out towards the unseen enemy, it was an ideal time for philosophical reflection, and my two hours of night duty were often lengthened consciously by half an hour, from the newness and intrigue of it all. (Though, in addition, I had by now lost my wristwatch – the only one in the squad – pilfered by some less philosophical comrade.) The visit of a British photographer and an

American movie cameraman was also an attraction one day, during which myself and about twenty others obligingly carried out a successful 'defence' against an 'enormous Red attack'.[43] Too good to last, the scene changed rapidly soon after, when a real 'Red attack' took place. Some enemy planes appeared, and dropped about twenty bombs. They were the first enemy planes I had seen and, like the militiamen, their aim was bad, all the bombs except one, which landed near the church, hitting well outside the village. The terrific height at which they were flying may have accounted for this.

The last day of October saw the issue of a *'rancho frío'* – cold rations – and the beginning of a push northwards. The village of Sevilla la Nueva, some ten kilometres away, was successfully occupied by midday, after slight opposition, and the advance was pushed on to Brunete, another five or six kilometres further north. In the open-country fighting between these two villages, a Portuguese volunteer from my company was taken prisoner. Some twenty minutes later, his still-warm body was discovered with his eyes, tongue, and worse, removed. With such tender treatment always facing them, the *Legionarios*, thanks probably to the restraining discipline under which they lived, confined their reprisals to the shooting of all prisoners. With the Red rabble still hurriedly retreating across the wide plain in the direction of El Escorial, the village of Brunete was evacuated by our troops and we returned to Navalcarnero. Our northern flank had been cleared, and Brunete itelf was permanently occupied some days later by Fascists from the Canary Islands, who with the Spanish Fascist troops of Morocco stood head and shoulders above the rest of the Fascist battalions.[44]

The musical band of the Legion arriving in Navalcarnero next day heartened us by the thought of the community singing we should have that evening, after finishing work on the trenches facing Madrid which we were enlargening and deepening. That evening and the next, the whole *bandera*, with the Moors and Spanish villagers forming an enthusiastic audience, formed a square around the band on the market place. We lustily roared through the repertoire of

Legion songs; the 'Marching Hymn'; the 'Sweetheart of Death'; the French *'La Madelon'* adapted to Spanish words, and ribald Spanish ballads – all rounded off by an adjournment to the taverns. We were blissfully unconscious that the morrow would see the beginning of a month's hard fighting, in which most soldiers present would become casualties, earning for them the distinction of being the first unit to force an entry into the boundaries of Madrid – a distinction which, no matter the result of the war, will remain an imperishable one for the *Sexta Bandera del Tercio*. The fault that the advantage and foothold gained therein was not taken up lies not at their door.

CHAPTER SEVEN

THE GREAT ADVANCE

A glance at the accompanying map [see p. 57] will show the position around Madrid on the day the advance began, 3 November 1936. The usefulness of the wedge driven into enemy territory at Navalcarnero served two purposes. It neutralized the country to the west of it, the Reds having to fall back on El Escorial, owing to the impossibility of munitioning this wild area once the main and only direct road from Madrid had been cut; and it provided the Nationalists with a fine main road leading direct from Talavera into Madrid, of which good use could be made. At 6.30 a.m. our three infantry companies, together with the Twenty-Third (Machine-Gun) Company, began to advance on the right of the road leading towards Móstoles, thirteen kilometres away. Supporting us were three companies of Moors to the left of the road, eleven light tanks and some six aeroplanes. Another Moorish company had been left behind in Navalcarnero as a rearguard. Our ten light field-artillery guns – a recent addition – followed us along the road some distance behind the troops advancing in extended order. Our way leading through vineyards, a thorough picnic of black grapes was enjoyed by all and sundry.

We reached the top of a small rise. On the far side of a valley where ran a river [the Guadarrama] twenty feet wide, but in which the water was only a foot deep, was a line of heavily wired defences. Behind this was a trench, in the centre of which a small farmhouse had been converted into a blockhouse by piles of sandbags. Not a shot being fired, but with fixed bayonets, we advanced cautiously down the slope and rising to the other side found this well-made fortification was entirely deserted – but only recently, as a still-smoking fire testified. Our movements had been watched from afar by scouts, and we had evidently been spotted advancing. The enemy, composed of regular army soldiers faithful to the Reds, and militiamen belonging to the private armies of the CNT, FAI and UGT – the only three Trade Unions of Spain, and of either Anarchist or extreme Left beliefs – were at this time completely demoralized by the constant defeats they suffered, and the big advances we made were always at the cost of heavy losses to them.[45] Brave enough when confronted by our regular or Fascist troops, but completely terror-stricken by the Legion or the Moors, the wonder is not that they so seldom fought back but they did not sue for surrender. Only strong-willed leaders kept them going until the arrival of the International Brigade which, giving them a 'Foreign Legion' of their own, restored their confidence in their cause.[46]

By eleven o'clock, the further eight kilometres to the village had been covered, and here we were met with the first opposition, the enemy being installed in the village houses.[47] Coming over a rise we ran into their fire almost before we knew the village was near. Our extended line became more so as we ran like deer down the slope to the thicket which offered sanctuary at the bottom. Two flanking movements carried out slowly, owing to the heavy fire of the defenders, threatened to surround the village, and we were soon in possession – the enemy beating a rapid retreat. A hurried search produced some pigeons, and a return to our billets saw the evening enlivened by a festive offering of *vino* with fried pigeons and potatoes. Some unknown friend left an almost new pipe in one of the houses, which enabled me to enjoy a smoke, while watching the evening change into night. For their part my rough-humoured *compañeros* gambled away the day's pickings, using a spread-out blanket as a card table.

Next morning the other three companies advanced five kilometres to the village of Alcorcón, while the Twenty-Fourth remained behind as a rearguard. We only went up to the new position to billet in the night, thus missing the morning's fun. Our comrades had surrounded some unfortunate militiamen in that village and, after a short siege, had taken it by storm. All the militiamen were not caught as next morning proved. In the neighbouring house to the one my section occupied was Kozma's *sección*, the First. As usual with such billets, a sentry was stationed outside the door. Just before dawn the sentry on duty hearing the closed door behind him opening, turned – to see a peasant. Giving the alarm instantly, and supported by the sentry on our doorstep, he took the man prisoner. The latter proved to be a militiaman who, finding the village surrounded, had thrown away his rifle and cartridge belt and, now to all appearances a peasant, had unluckily chosen as his refuge a dwelling later chosen as a billet. Miraculously undiscovered the previous night, owing to it being dark when we occupied the houses, he had thought it safe to vacate his hiding place before dawn, stepping over the sleeping soldiers to reach the door, and evidently not realising that a sentry would be posted. Masquerading as a non-combatant, according to international law he could be treated as a spy, and accordingly a firing party soon 'liquidated' him.

We remained at Alcorcón for that day – during which the village station with a rail-car and single tickets (returns were unpopular) to Madrid gave us endless fun – and continued the advance the following morning. This time we exchanged sides of the road with the Moors. A stuffed leopard found in the village and appropriated by *Teniente* Ivanoff, was packed onto the company's lorry to follow behind us as a mascot – only to be jettisoned within twenty-four hours in a roadside ditch, upon the death of the said *Teniente*.

CHAPTER EIGHT

CRUDE DEATH

Backed by far more artillery than we possessed, their air power about equal to ours, the enemy were awaiting us.[48] Although under heavy shell-fire, we managed to advance and, after taking a line of trenches by storm, we continued our advance in a crescent-shaped extended formation, with the two points reaching forward of the centre. Soon we were overlooking a valley where the enemy were hidden by the low scrub covering the valley bed. This gave some of them an opportunity to escape but our fire, falling on them from three sides, killed and wounded many.

We slackened fire and descended into the valley. Soon the prisoners began to be gathered in. The wounded were shot, usually in the stomach – it was only a few days since we had seen the mutilated body of the Portuguese. The unwounded prisoners met a similar end, after a preliminary examination. *Teniente* Dmitri Ivanoff of my company, a bluff, bearded Bulgarian giant, with many years of service in this Legion and its French counterpart behind him, was in temporary command of the company, since our captain was now acting *comandante* of the *bandera*. Ivanoff had a batch of twenty-five prisoners brought before him. A hurried examination of them was terminated with the rattle of the sub machine-gun – the only one in the *bandera* – which he possessed. Grim retribution, in the shape of an enemy shell, struck him that same afternoon, blowing off his legs, and resulting in his death. Ivanoff was brutal but a man for all that, possessing a frame of iron and enough courage to have taken his section to storm the gates of Hades if ordered to do so. One bearded militiaman I saw was shot three times; first in the stomach, by my sergeant for hesitating over his answers to questions as to his political beliefs; secondly, by my corporal, in the same place; and the misericordia was given him through the brain by a squad-mate to end his sufferings.[49]

These last illustrations – typical of many – showed the two types, the one brutalized by years of warfare against the barbaric Moor, and the other, a younger generation recruited since the Civil War began. Both the NCOs involved were kind and generous comrades – but a world of sentiment separated them.[50]

Now we were only a few kilometres from the city outskirts. But alongside the road we lay for three hours, returning the heavy fire from the double line of trenches commencing three hundred yards away. Their artillery kept bothering us, as did an armoured train which, the railway track into Madrid being only a hundred yards to the right, kept shelling us at short range. The slopes of the valley protected us somewhat, and at last we saw that the first line of the trenches had been given up. The armoured train also having retreated, which particularly pleased my *escuadra* (having been allotted the job of guarding the road and thus being the nearest to the infernal thing), we rose with fixed bayonets to charge the second line. Crossing the first line without any difficulty we found the second line also empty and carrying on the pursuit, entered the permanent military camp of Carabanchel Alto.[51] Before the war an encampment for infantry and artillery, this had evidently been chosen as a site for a desperate resistance. Indeed, it could have even broken us, given better defenders, as we were only about eleven hundred men all told, and without reserves (the nearest were in Navalcarnero, twenty kilometres away) against the easily outnumbering forces Madrid could, and did, throw against us. The trenches were the best-constructed I ever saw, full of enfilading angles, and with zig-zag communication trenches leading back to the second line trench. However 'the best laid schemes . . .', and with only moderate casualties, we rushed in.

Taking no chances in a place honeycombed with barracks buildings we charged through it and into the civilian areas, along the main street, throwing bombs into suspicious-looking places before searching them, while the Moors came in from their side.[52]

CRUDE DEATH

During this search, we found the half-burnt body of the parish priest, his little church nearby turned into a Communist Hall, the cross above the door replaced by the hammer and sickle done in red paint, and the doors and walls defaced by slogans, lewdness and the initials of various political parties. Religious persecution, 1936 vintage. How little distant we were, after all, from the Inquisition, Torquemada, the Crusades and Jesus Christ.[53]

Nothing too threatening discovered, we settled down in style to billets in the nearby radio station, with nice beds of mattresses from the deserted villas. On the second day of our stay in Madrid, Sunday 8 November – notable also for the last wash I was to have for three weeks – we advanced out of Carabanchel into the former Royal Park, the famous Casa de Campo, entering through breaches blown in the twelve-foot high walls. In this vast hunting park of the former kings of Spain, we were seemingly entirely lost, being surrounded with huge trees and tangled undergrowth, interspersed with clearings and streams, with roads leading off in all directions. Bursting from a thicket, we nearly dropped upon a huge Russian tank, containing a rapid-fire cannon, on the road below us. Before the surprised occupants even realised our presence, its inside was on fire, the result of bottles of petrol – each *escuadra* carried a bottle for these purposes – followed by equally well-directed bombs being flung at the loopholes in the tank.[54]

Grateful to get through this dangerous park, open as we had been there to ambush, we eventually took up positions on a bluff overlooking the Rio Manzanares. Above and on the other side of the river, only a quarter of a mile away, began central Madrid, city of one million inhabitants, capital of Spain, and our objective. Victory seemed within our grasp yet, looking across at the great city spreading across the top of that high plateau, it seemed it might swallow by its vastness our small force. An ominous sign were the already blown-up bridges crossing the river, which meant a hotly contested passage through the waters.[55]

CHAPTER NINE

THE PASSAGE OF THE RIO MANZANARES

An exact week passed.[56] Despite the tall trees hiding the sun, we were awoken early each morning. Although I now had two blankets (my *capote* had been 'scrounged' in Navalcarnero by some individual unknown) the white frost gathered thickly on our bedclothes and slowly soaked through to our skins. The days slipped by with nothing to do except gaze at our goal across the river, and put up with the air raids constantly launched against us. During these, several combats took place between planes of both sides resulting in the never-to-be-forgotten sight of falling planes on fire or out of control. Several night-attacks against us by militia took place also, but were beaten off, although assisted by heavy Russian tanks.

Sunday 15 November – the High Command were just beginning the Sunday-attack principle, probably believing in the more potent efficacy of the saints on that day – saw the commencement of the big attack. Great preparations for the advance were made, including a week's aerial bombardment of the enemy positions, and the allotment to each company of precise objectives, as it might have meant otherwise the taking of wrong roads, streets or even cul-de-sacs. For this purpose, each officer carried large-scale maps. Don Luis Aranda Mata, brother to the famous general of Oviedo-defence fame, was still acting *comandante* of the whole *bandera*, while a lieutenant from Toledo had replaced Ivanoff in temporary command of the Twenty-Fourth. We formed up, company by company, in the thick woods beneath the trenches, which had been taken over by a battalion of Fascists from Morocco before dawn.[57] We had to our immediate left a *tabor* of Moors; to the right, another *tabor*, with the Seventh *Bandera* further over, and opposite the Royal Palace, having earlier advanced from Toledo. Yet further to the south-east were other Moorish *tabors* and the Fourth *Bandera* – the latter on the Córdoba road – which though not interested directly in the day's operations, served to keep the enemy away from our flank.

Zero-hour came, and to the screams of artillery and trench mortar shells, and the heavy concussions of the bombs dropped by the twenty-three German three-engined Junkers overhead – the first time we had ever seen them – Madrid awoke from a dreamy dawn into vigilance. Incidentally, these bombers were protected by fourteen scouts [i.e., fighters] also of German origin. 'Non-intervention' was already at work on both sides; on ours, with a few tanks and aeroplanes, on the other side, with the many powerful Russian tanks, both of the heavy, cannon-bearing type, and also the light machine-gun varieties.[58]

The enemy's guns opened up in answer to ours, but company after company in numerical order and extended lines began to run across the bare plain leading to the river. Exposed to view, within easy range, man after man could be seen dropping. We were glad when it came our company's turn to get off the mark, although being the last company numerically of the *bandera*, it meant going through a zone now swept by the bullets of a thoroughly awakened enemy. Between us and the river was the high wall which surrounds the vast acreage of the Royal Park, in which breaches had, days previously, been blown. Halfway to the wall was a royal stables – our first resting-place. The first section gaining this and going on to near the gapped wall in front, mine – the second – ran for the building. It contained only empty loose boxes bedecked with photographs of late denizens and even their horseshoes mounted on small shields.[59] Our turn now came again and we dashed to the breach in the wall. Here, our captain ordered the section to divert to a shooting box with a coloured brick tower, known to us as the '*casa colorada*', in the centre of the open parkland to our immediate left. The Moors had been held up here by a body of the enemy strongly entrenched in the copse which lay further on, and it now became necessary for my *bandera* to put out a flank-guard in this direction to protect those who were already across the river. Our job was to take this position at any cost.

A hurried dash under crossfire from the heights and the hidden enemy in front, who could see our objective immediately, got us into precarious safety inside the building, with the exception of one *Sevillano* – the squad-mate who had given the misericordia to the dying militiaman at Alcorcón – who staggered in wounded by a bullet which had entered just above the right hip. The miracle had been that he and others (I was directly behind him) had not been blown up. Like all of us, he was wearing a bomb-thrower's belt containing six live bombs, the case of which is only made of thin tin, and if the bullet had struck him a few inches more to the right or left a bomb would have exploded. However, for him, the result was the same, death coming almost immediately.

The interior of the shooting box was tiled and panelled, and when the evening came, and the pressure was slightly eased, the Moors having driven the enemy back, the place looked like a recently excavated Egyptian relic. In their efforts to dislodge us, the enemy mortars in the city above, and one with the group in front of us, had battered the place almost to pieces. The tower had partially collapsed onto the single-floored building beneath, adding to the casualties. To make things worse for us, the enemy had set the undergrowth between their trench and the house on fire, and the flames had rolled quite near. However, the wind changed, and the flames ironically swept back upon the 'fire bugs' themselves.

In the gathering dusk, we handed over our still-unconquered position to a party of Moors, and crossing back to the wall climbed through the breach, to find the river only a few yards away. A descent down the steep bank on our side enabled us to cross on foot, the water being only knee high, and mounting again on the other side, we arrived at the *Bandera* HQ. Near this position was a park where we slept out that night. The rest of the company and the whole *bandera*, under continuous fire, had already crossed the exposed river and established themselves above us, well within the University City.[60]

Naturally, our lorries were unable to bring up the cooks. I should mention here that each company has its own cooks and entirely separate kitchen, being so constituted as to be able to operate quite independently from the rest if necessary. In action, the convention is that field kitchens are convoyed by one-third of the machine-gun company (i.e. eight guns) whose personnel are then fed by the company being served. (Several examples of this procedure occurred during my service, in one instance where my company had been sent to a front fifteen miles from the rest.) On the first day in the University City, besides having to dine on a tin of sardines, bread and sausage, washed down with river water, we had no blankets, these having been piled aboard the lorries to give us extra mobility during the day's action. With breeches and boots soaked through, unable to light fires for fear of the numerous enemy trench mortars above us, we passed a sleepless night, almost frozen with the cold and grumbling at our lucky comrades installed (even if without blankets) in buildings in the darkness above us.[61]

The Nationalists were at last the right side of the river, but the stretcher-bearers were beginning to pass with their burdens from above. The casualty roll had begun to mount, to be enormously swollen in the next three weeks. Our own *escuadra* was two short already, another man having been wounded by a shell splinter in the *'casa colorada'*, leaving only three of us to do the duty of five. Furthermore the cold food mentioned above, doubled, became our daily rations until a plank bridge was finished across the river a week later, enabling the lorries to cross. Meanwhile, our iron rations and blankets were brought over the river by mules before the dawn.[62]

CHAPTER TEN

THE UNIVERSITY CITY[63]

The dawn saw my section running through the sloping park to the Faculty of Medicine, the heel of my corporal's boot being torn off by a bullet – our only casualty! The building was large, distinctive and modern, like most of the buildings in this suburb of hospitals, asylums,

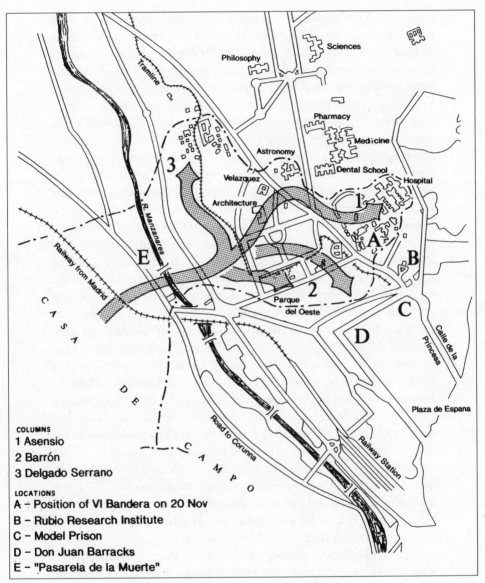

Sciences

Philosophy

Pharmacy

Medicine

Astronomy

Dental School

Velazquez

Hospital

Architecture

Tramline

R. Manzanares

Railway from Madrid

3

1

A

B

E

C A S A

2

Parque del Oeste

C

D

Calle de la Princesa

D E

Road to Corunna

Plaza de Espana

C A M P O

Railway Station

COLUMNS
1 Asensio
2 Barrón
3 Delgado Serrano

LOCATIONS
A – Position of VI Bandera on 20 Nov
B – Rubio Research Institute
C – Model Prison
D – Don Juan Barracks
E – "Pasarela de la Muerte"

The attack on Madrid via the University City, November 1936.

colleges and the university were.[64] A short pause here, and we were off again to the nearby Casa de Velázquez – a French-built college, erected in 1928 for *Hautes Études* and Fine Arts – where the rest of the company and some Moors were already installed. Evidently untouched by the usual looting mobs of Communists, because of its French diplomatic protection, it was soon to undergo different trials.

A series of stone steps led up to its magnificent cloistered patio, now occupied by the company mules. Inside, to the strains of the latest Spanish 'hits' from a gramophone, our companions were busily searching the studios and apartments of its late occupants, several lucky strikes being made. Three thousand pesetas was one man's luck, while a Moor smashed open a safe to find several thousand franc notes – to be cheated out of half of them by a Spanish corporal who explained they were 'duds'! Its priceless library was not even spared, many of the books, including sixteenth-century histories of France, having been torn off the shelves to build barricades in the glassless windows. Small cases of museum pieces had been broken open for the antique gold and silver inside. Looting was the unofficial order of the day, and even some of the officers were guilty of it. I myself stole, for that is what it amounts to even though permitted or at least unrestrained, a small collection of ancient Spanish coins of Phoenician, Roman, Moorish and Armada vintage, while the more scrupulous Kozma appropriated a stamp collection. *'In vino veritas'* is an old tag but even cold sober, having only water to drink, environment and lawless opportunity would strain the conscience of a saint.[65]

Two days passed pleasantly, apart from attacks on us each night from adjacent buildings in enemy hands; pleasantly, that is, if one omits the sardines, and the water from the basins of a small fountain out of which the mules also drank, and in which the Moors, until very forcibly restrained, made their ablutions.

A forward advance, during which most of the unfortunate mules were killed, brought us to the huge National Institute of Hygiene and Sanitation. It was about this time [18 November] that the first of the International Battalions came into operation.[66] Where obviously Spanish militiamen were previously opposed to us, prisoners and dead of (equally obviously) foreign derivation began to crop up. Speaking from actual experience, the Spanish militiamen would not and could not have put on the stiff counter-attacks which came regularly about an hour after nightfall. However, inside huge, thick-walled buildings as we were, the attacks failed quite as regularly, with heavy losses to the enemy. Their objective was that of clearing us out of the suburb before we had time to settle down, but their only effect was the useful practice it gave us with our rifles and bombs, besides temporarily cutting off each building's communication with the outside world.

Furthermore it was easy for our sentries to spot the attack for, apart from its regular timing, the dynamite bombs which they hurled when within range, which was often almost to the windows, had to be lit with matches, and so it was usual to see pin-pricks of light spring up out of the darkness. Midnight meant relaxation for, the moon rising, it meant even surer suicide to attack with our heavy machine-guns securely perched on the flat roof tops. Indeed, the enemy artillery and trench mortars (the latter used at long range as if light artillery), caused us far more annoyance. The Casa de Velázquez, for example, was almost destroyed by them during our two-day occupation and the very next day the by-then empty building was set on fire and razed to the ground by their aircraft.

Several days' stay in the Hygiene Institute saw us now faced with a major problem. The supply of cigarette papers had run out, while tobacco could only be bought off the Moors at six times its normal price. Ordinary paper not proving very successful, the only fortunate ones were the pipe-smokers, mainly foreigners, as only the aged smoke pipes in Spain. Luckily I still had my pipe of Móstoles days. This unfortunate state lasted until our relief, except for one small consignment of cigarettes subscribed for by the officers and given us. (Incidentally, will the director of the late Casa de Velázquez accept my grateful thanks for a half-full box of cigars kindly left behind?)

The end of the first week in University City saw another dash, past several asylums, to the Parque del Oeste. My company occupied a children's orthopaedic hospital, long since deserted by the children, the Twenty-First a house down below us, with less than four hundred yards further on to the south the Cárcel Modelo, gigantic prison and now strongly held enemy fortress. The Twenty-Second Company were somewhere to our left and the machine-gun company split up between us. From our position, we were looking down the mile-long Calle de la Princesa, running into the heart of Madrid. About a quarter of the way down – where a main street running from the Mint crossed it – a sandbag barricade had been built across it, and behind this light field-guns and mortars had been placed.[67]

The bridge finished, hot food was now coming up to us again.[68] Communication trenches leading back from the Hospital to the Asilo, being used as a kitchen, had also been rapidly constructed. One day's menu at this time was one small ladle of coffee for breakfast; boiled rice, a fried sausage, a quarter-kilo of bread, coffee and vino at midday; soup, boiled haricots, bread, coffee and *vino* at about 5.30 p.m. The water having been cut off by the enemy, there was none obtainable so that we could only refresh ourselves at meal times, quite long enough intervals in the heat of the daytimes, while washing was entirely out of the question.

The days passed with sentry duty and the digging of communication trenches between the buildings, while the regular attack each night kept us busy. One night, Kozma and I were the guards given to the cooks who always went (after the routine attack) down to the Twenty-First below us with *vino* and iron rations, these unfortunates being entirely cut off from food and verbal communication during the daytime. This was a vivid experience, as it meant crossing and re-crossing the Parque del Oeste in the short period left before the rising of the moon, with the Reds only three hundred yards away, and the possibility of meeting enemy patrols. To complicate matters, we stayed talking to a White Russian we knew in that company for too long, and found the cooks had been in such a hurry to return that they had gone without us. We did not know the password, and had to approach the captain for it, but were not yet out of our troubles, for on our return, the sentries having been changed in our absence, we were subjected to an interrogation before being admitted, our foreign intonations having aroused their suspicion. The sounds of the conversation being carried on the still night air, the enemy forthwith opened up in our direction with machine-guns, adding to our discomfort. The later recriminations of our companions – the whole of the company having been aroused to repel this supposed attack – did not help matters.

Only one other time did I hear the big doors barred behind me at night. This was when my corporal, myself and a squad-mate were detailed to bury an enemy major, shot outside a window a week previously and now getting a little high; the first and only enemy I ever saw being buried, a state of things which will inevitably lead to plagues if not corrected. He was at the side of the hospital furthest from the enemy and, the moon being well up, it was with nervous irritability at each other's alleged lack of digging power that my comrade and I began to dig, the corporal keeping his rifle at the ready for possible enemy patrols. Digging finished, the body proved to be too big for the hole, but forcible conversion being made, leaving only an inch of soil above the corpse, everything ended satisfactorily for everybody concerned.

A week's stay saw us, again on a Sunday, ready for attacking the Cárcel Modelo, an attack eagerly awaited as we were plastered at regular intervals where we were by the enemy guns. This occurred especially at midday, when they spotted the cooks arriving with our food, owing to the latter being unavoidably exposed at one stage of their journey. I can quite assuredly say that brick dust in one's soup and beans is not conducive to brotherly love towards one's enemies.

CHAPTER ELEVEN

MORTAL ESSAY

The Cárcel Modelo, model prison of Madrid, was emptied of its criminals by the mobs at the beginning of the civil war and later restocked with opponents, both of politics and class. Among these was the late José Antonio Primo de Rivera, chief of the Falange de las JONS (Phalanx of Young National Socialist Workers), the Spanish Fascist party, who was unfortunately in Madrid when the movement against the Government began. Our occupation of the nearby Casa de Campo saw the hurried shooting in batches of the unfortunate prisoners to prevent successful release. Valuable individual hostages such as José Antonio were taken to prisons on the Mediterranean coast. He himself was taken to Málaga, being later shot there, to prevent his release by our advancing troops. The prison had then been converted into a well-defended fortress, as was a nearby barracks.[69]

The only possible approach for us lay through the open Parque del Oeste, so that we were certain of a warm reception. It should here be mentioned, bearing importantly on the matter as it does, that a low parapet ran along the edge of the thirty-foot drop between us and the lower level in front – on which the house occupied by the Twenty-First, and the prison, both lay. The only descent was via an asphalt drive leading up to one end of the parapet. To the sound and sight of the exploding shells fired at an oblique angle to our advance by our artillery in the Casa de Campo, the Twenty-Second left their position to our left, passed around the side of ours, and, hugging the parapet as long as possible, dashed down the bullet-swept road to the house below – which was to be their final jumping-off point. Immediately they had passed us, our company started to follow, *pelotón* by *pelotón*, the machine-gun company being left in position in order to cover our advance.

The first section getting off down the drive, my *pelotón* – the first of the second section – went out to the parapet ready to follow as soon as possible. The position was now as follows. The remnants of the Twenty-First, whose habitation had been terrifically bombarded in the past week, causing very heavy casualties, were lying out near the prison; the Twenty-Second were in occupation of the house; the first section of our company lying out between the house and the hospital; my *pelotón* sheltering behind the parapet; our companion *pelotón* and the last section of the Twenty-Fourth still inside the hospital.

At this point, the same aerial fleet that had helped us to cross the Manzanares appeared, late, owing probably to faulty staff work, and circled once around overhead to get its bearings properly. Bombs then commenced raining on the barracks to the west of the prison, then on the prison itself, and finally ON US! A tragic and unfortunate blunder had been made – we said worse at the time – throwing away our fair chances of taking the prison and thus the entrance and possible capture of Madrid proper. It is not for me to express an opinion on the reason for it. I only know the actual result, for which, on behalf of my dead *compañeros*, I hope someone was shot.

The *bandera* had received its last reinforcements at Navalcarnero but until the advance from the Casa de Campo had suffered little loss, and we would then have been roughly 550 men. Since that day, 15 November, casualties had been heavy so that we were now seriously short of men, even on the morning of this attack. The losses passing down that bullet-swept drive can be imagined as can those occasioned by the enemy artillery who were firing at almost point-blank range. The bombardment by our own aeroplanes thus left us in such state that only retreat was possible which was accordingly carried out, the Twenty-Second remaining below until nightfall, so as to lessen casualties on their return up that cursed drive.

Back inside the hospital my company took stock of its remnants. My own *escuadra* the previous night four, and a fortnight earlier six strong, consisted now of only myself and one other, the corporal having been wounded and another member killed. Kozma, fortunately, was safe, while Frantisek, who had broken his glasses through falling asleep on sentry duty at the Casa de Velázquez, and had been transferred to the remnants of the mule column instead of suffering the death penalty he was liable to, had not been concerned in the day's events. A similar state existed everywhere, with in two instances whole *escuadras* having disappeared. A rapid reorganization took place, giving us two; the company trumpeter, José Espí, as corporal, and a *Sevillano* as a third private. Even so, we were even then still as badly off as ever, each individual still having two hours on and four off as sentry duty, day and night.[70]

Another week in the hospital, of which we were now heartily sick, saw our relief at dusk on 5 December by a *tabor* of Moors; the *bandera's* evacuation leading it down through the deep and lorry-wide communication trench being constructed by engineers, to the sound of whose valedictory congratulations, and the firing from the usual attack now broken out behind us, we crossed the plank bridge over the river. Once safely over, we marched all the way to Leganés before entraining for Talavera de la Reina – a battle-scarred remnant of only 127 men. Casualties had been seventy-seven per cent of our strength of three weeks earlier.[71]

CHAPTER TWELVE
ADVENTURES AND EXCURSIONS

Our arrival in Talavera was followed in a day or so, and after the issue of clean clothes, then a bath and shave, by a parade before Colonel Yagüe, chief of the Legion. To the cheers of the populace and the stirring strains of 'The Volunteers' March' we marched past the saluting base, not as a remnant of a *bandera* but as a complete one, with the places of the dead and wounded being left blank, for they had well earned the right to be *'presente'*, if only in the spirit. Here the whole file of an *escuadra* would be missing; there an officer, sergeant or corporal, but the march-past proceeded with its lines and files in as good order, as if it were a normal parade. Every man's heart was set on doing his utmost in honour of our missing comrades. My own *escuadra* showed gaps for the corporal and the three other casualties. The bestowing of the *Medalla Militar* to the *bandera* collectively and the companies individually was followed by a banquet in our honour, altogether a memorable day's experience.

The receipt of fresh recruits was immediate. For a few hurried days they licked them into shape, then once more we passed the saluting base and the Colonel, this time restored to full strength. The same afternoon, I was one of the Guard of Honour at the funeral of a Legion captain killed on the Madrid front and brought to Talavera for burial. Two files marched in slow time behind the black-plumed horses and hearse with rifles stiffly held at the shoulder, succeeded by a quick march and salute past the coffin at the cemetery gates, to the strains of the Legion March; which, followed by the thankfully received 'at ease' return walk, constituted an honour (in our opinion) fit for any general!

With these exceptions our days in Talavera were spent in concentrated training, especially in parade ground drill. I had seen the effect of our disciplined troops against numerically superior but undisciplined enemy ones. Discipline destroys self-reliance to some extent but a man who is used to doing as his NCOs and officers do is not the one to fail at the last ditch, like an undisciplined man will at the first. With good training, as long as the leaders do not fail, often the last ditch, however impregnable it may look, is crossed with ease.

I was now accounted a seasoned veteran, and treated as such, being excused barrack fatigues, for there were plenty of *quintos* about on the parade ground. Yet I showed up badly at this time, having previously only had half a day's parade drill back in October, an invidious position which (however) was successfully rectified before the end of the month.

The ninth day of our stay in Talavera saw the reorganization of the *bandera*, *escuadras* and *pelotones* being finally made up to strength, *'quintos'* having, until now, been separated from *'veteranos'* – the sheep from the wolves, as it were. They had (however) been previously initiated into the mysteries of *'seis y media'* and *'monte'*, lining our pockets in the process, although the old soldier secrets were kept from the innocent children – some of whom were rapidly approaching middle-age! I had remained with Cabo Espí in the Second Section during this reorganization, but my other comrades had been redistributed to another *escuadra*. There were simply insufficient *veteranos* to leave even two together, except in the important First Section, while some *escuadras* had none at all apart from the *cabos* in the Third Section. The rest of our new *escuadra* consisted of a *toreador* (bullfighter), and farm labourer, and a Portuguese – the latter the most animal-like person probably ever known, stupid and gross, too slow-witted to resent a wrong but, paradoxically, quick to appreciate a kindness.

The same afternoon we left by train for Bargas, whence a short journey by road would bring us to Toledo. On the train, a minor sensation ran the whole length of the company. The Czech, Frantisek Shostek, had deserted! Still without his glasses, he had nevertheless been restored to the company from the mule column, and had boarded the train with the rest of us. Leaving his equipment and rifle on the rack he had made an excuse to leave the compartment, stepped down on the side of the coach furthest from the platform, and disappeared! In the way honoured by tradition, his loss was not discovered until the train was well away from Talavera, and the news had to be telegraphed back.

Shostek's Genoese exploits will be recalled by the reader. During our first stay in Navalcarnero he had gone to the *bandera* doctor with regard to VD. He had been given a prescription for the local chemist who was still practising in the village, but the price was prohibitive with his small pay, and failing to get other satisfaction from the doctor, things had gone from bad to worse with him. In the University City, Kozma and I provided an audience for his justified grouses. A Portuguese fellow-sufferer at Navalcarnero had been sent to hospital, having become so badly affected as to have been unable to walk.

Frantisek, afraid of permanent effects on his health, had discussed with us the prospects of successful desertion but we had tried to dissuade him from it, harping on the certain firing squad which awaited his first slip. I should have mentioned that at the Talavera recruiting depot where I had first known him, he had not been a recruit, but had been brought in as having missed the train which had just taken the Fourth *Bandera* up to the front. He had been strongly suspected then of attempted desertion and another failed attempt could have but one result. In Talavera he had borrowed money from everyone and with the proceeds he got clean away this time, but we were told by the company clerk in January that he had been caught down south and placed in the military prison at Cádiz. That was the last we ever heard of him, and the end of the story can only be conjectured.

Although Kozma and I had not been expecting this move of his, we had to sympathize, as, though he had tried all sorts of dodges to get sent to hospital, they had failed. The doctor, unreasonably, looked upon the lack of treatment as a punishment, instead of clearing him out as a possible source of infection to the rest of us. His was not an isolated case, as periodical medical inspections – if they had ever been held – would have disclosed. My own corporal, Espí (as I learned after his death in February) was another sufferer; this sort of thing could only be expected with the *vivandières* about, who were allowed to live with sergeants and others, even following us into the front-line. The tragedy that messing as we often did on common plates left innocent persons open to infection through unawareness of another's ill health.[72]

Toledo, where we were now quartered in the Escuela de los Maestros, knew us for a further seven days, which I took advantage of during time off with visits to the battered remnants of the Alcázar. This had been the scene of an epic defence at the commencement of hostilities. Surrounded in this high and massive-walled citadel, a small force of Nationalists held out for seventy-two days against the whole surrounding Red army, undergoing constant mine explosions and heavy shelling. The miracle is not that the building is ruined but that even the ruins exist. It is remarkable that any of the defenders managed to live to greet the relieving force – the Fifth *Bandera*, I believe – still unconquered. Decorations and promotions were immediately and justifiably showered upon them. Allowing for a certain amount of other destruction, mostly in the Alcázar district, notably Cervantes' Posada de la Sangre, Toledo has not been so terrifically damaged. Its narrow, medieval streets provided us with pleasantness and refreshment, which we were sorry to leave for Boadilla del Monte, a small village north of the Alcorcón–Madrid road to which we moved shortly before Christmas Day.[73]

December 24 is the main fiesta day in Spain and for dinner we received special food. Rice boiled in olive oil with meat, a fish course and turkey with tomato made up the menu. An apple, a cigar, *vino* and coffee with a tot of brandy for each man polished off our banquet. Another good meal at night saw the second issue of *vino* and brandy, for the usual marking of Christmas Eve, and a riotous time was had by everybody – one sergeant being so riotous as to be confined to quarters and eventually transferred to another *bandera*.

On Christmas Day, I overheard an incoming order to set the men digging trenches to the east of the village. Here there was no front as such, an enormous No-Man's-Land running out to the enemy positions in the Guadarramas. But these trenches were actually occupied a few days later by Spanish Regular Infantry, to protect our rear – as will be seen. However, I was determined not to work on my Bank Holiday and so set off to the ancient monastery in the village. In this monastery were then quartered some Germans and Roumanians of the Twenty-First Company, the latter a delegation of solidarity from the 'Iron Guards', recruits who had joined us on our return to Talavera.[74] In the company of some of these, I had a look around inside to see the damage wreaked by the enemy; the crucifixes all torn down and burned, the altar and interior of the church befouled, the priceless records and manuscripts scattered everywhere, even in the streets of the village. One document I noticed bore the signature of Philip II and dealt with the award of land to the monastery. The neighbouring palace,

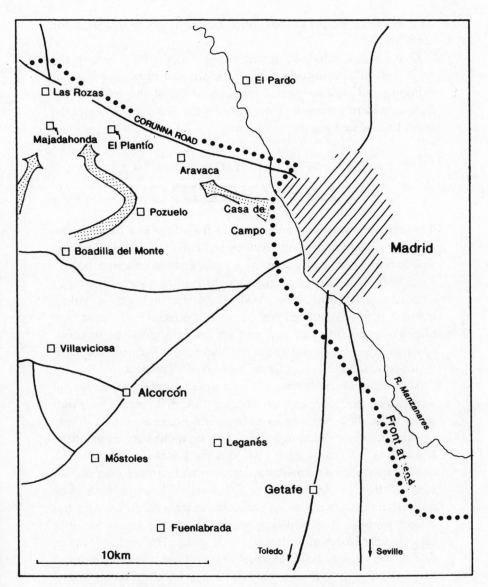

The battles for the Corunna Road, winter 1936–7.

with its private chapel of some titled family, had been treated in the same way.[75]

One comical interlude in this village was the discovery, in the deep well of a farmyard from which we had been drawing our drinking and washing water for some days, of the body of the farmer, evidently thrown down there by the Reds. No wonder the water had seemed strange to the taste!

CHAPTER THIRTEEN
DISTINGUIDO

The 1 January saw us advancing out of the village in a Madrid-wise direction under cover of our artillery and tanks.[76] The thick hunting woods across our course gave us a limited range of vision but we successfully passed the enemy trench, finding there all sorts of delicacies left from New Year's Eve. Further on, a young militiawoman of seventeen was captured, wounded in the posterior. She was given first aid, and sent off under a guard to Boadilla. Quixotic treatment compared to the shooting of her male comrades which soon followed – but Spain is a land of incongruity.[77]

That night saw us sleeping out in a wooded valley 'somewhere in Spain'. The next day, another advance took us across barren plains to an unfinished highway or railway embankment with a deeply rutted road of sorts running parallel with it on our side, leading from Boadilla to Las Rozas. Here, we took up positions, digging small holes into the embankment for sleeping and defence purposes. It was well that we did so, for the following midday an attack burst forth from the woods a quarter of a mile in front of us. We were not caught napping, and well-directed fire drove the enemy infantry back into the woods after they had only gone a few yards. However, four or five Russian heavy-cannon tanks in front of them continued to come on. Two anti-tank gun units we had with us fought a duel with them – though we had to kick the gunners' backsides to make

General Millan Astray.

General Miguel Cabanellas.

Peter Kemp in legionary uniform.

Nationalist Army:
1 Sargento porta-guión, 2ª Bandera, Spanish Foreign Legion;
   summer campaign dress, 1936-37
2 Legionario de 1ª clase, Spanish Foreign Legion; winter
   campaign dress, 1938
3 Teniente, infantry, summer campaign dress

Spanish foreign legion: emblems, flags and uniforms.

*Lieutenant Colonel Asensio Cabanillas,
commander of FHT's column.*

Officers of the VI Bandera after the capture of Navalcarnero, October 1936.

FHT in trenches near Navalcarnero, 21 October 1936.

A legionary bandera *advances towards Madrid, October 1936.*

The University City after the failure of the Nationalist attack on Madrid, winter 1936–7.

Legionary recruits entraining at Talavera.

The village of San Martín de la Vega under fire during the battle of Jarama, February 1937.

Frank in Talavera after the battle of Toledo, May 1937.

Frank today wearing the gorillo *forage cap.*

General O'Duffy as Brigadier-Inspector of the XV
Bandera del Tercio.

Tom McMullen and comrades arriving home in Dublin, June 1937.

The first day of the battle of Brunete, 6 July 1937. Republican troops are advancing towards Villanueva de la Canada.

them do it. Bullets meanwhile were also poured into the woods to warn the enemy what to expect if they broke cover again. Halting half-way between us, the tanks began to methodically pelt us with steel, but their ammunition seeming to run out, they eventually retreated. This was fortunate for us, for although we had the bombs and petrol ready for them we were without barbed-wire defences, which are a comforting although useless ally against tanks.[78] For help given to the anti-tank guns and other things, I came out of this affair *'distinguido'* — distinguished, mentioned in orders — a sure step to promotion, and so I was quite content with the day's work.

Several days passed, and we at last began to advance on the wooded country in front of us. Quick dashes through the low bushes soon brought us to the woods. A high tower with a cupola containing a machine-gun nest interrupted our progress, until our artillery shells dropped too near for their comfort, its occupants fleeing. Inside the woods the line of trenches had been abandoned, as had cases of Russian tinned meats and paste. During a brief rest period these were broached and our rations of sardines and sausages exchanged for these Communist delicacies, with pious thanks to Comrade Stalin for his generosity.

The woods seemed to stretch for miles and, although we had not seen an enemy soldier yet, they had not a long start in front of us. At last the woods came to an end and, after having passed four lines of enemy trenches, we were suddenly greeted by the familiar 'tut-tut-tut' of the Russian machine-guns used by the other side. They were lying in a fifth line of trenches, outside Pozuelo — a summer resort for Madrid's foreign population. While the rest of the *bandera* and an accompanying *tabor* of Moors kept up a reply to the enemy fire, my own company, by a flanking movement, burst into the town. Threatened with encirclement, the Reds immediately beat a hurried retreat — some, not knowing where the danger at their rear lay, running right into our hands. Some staff officers, trying to escape in a motor car, also dropped into our clutches. A tragic, half-understood event took place when a small body of the enemy, retiring in orderly fashion, saw us barring their road. Upon seeing us in front of his men, the captain in charge of them advanced alone and, taking out his pistol, shot himself through the head, crying out as he did so *'¡Arriba España!'* – the political slogan and password of *our* side. Evidently he was a just man, who regarded himself as responsible for the safety of the men he led, and yet could not bring himself to honestly lead them against us, being (to judge from his dying words) one of the many officers who were forced at pistol point to lead their men against Franco on the beginning of hostilities.

Pozuelo, on the main Madrid road to Corunna, boasted a stone memorial recently erected and marked 'They shall not pass'. This pointed up the failure of two previous *banderas* to take or keep the town.[79] The place also provided us with real luxury, not only in the form of blankets from the fine holiday villas plentifully dotted about, but also more Russian provisions; this time including cooked hams and butter, tobacco, cigarettes and even champagne, the gift of 'the workers' to the 'People's Army'. In all, a tolerable exposition of the comfort to be derived from legalized Communism. Large stores of arms munitions and medical supplies made its capture even more noteworthy, for which the Sixth *Bandera* earned another collective *Medalla Militar*, while my company got an extra one just for itself.

My section took up positions in two adjoining villas on the outskirts of the town. There we received, on the first night, the full force of a counter-attack, which was beaten off after the enemy had come right up to the outside walls of the villa, where our bombs came at once into play. One wounded adversary lingered on in the darkness outside for several hours, calling his *'camaradas'* to come back and assist him. We were not so foolish as to go out for him as it might have been a trap. Apparently, however, his *'camaradas'* were miles away, and his calls growing fainter and fainter, eventually ceased with death's merciful approach. It is scenes like this which stick in the mind; a dying man who calls not political slogans, but useless appeals to his comrades and his mother – the loneliness of Death which is, sometimes, War. Yet only a few days earlier, during the tank attack, a seriously wounded Mexican *legionario* called out to the *compañeros* he was leaving, '¡*Viva España, Viva la Legíon, Viva la Muerte!*'. This contrasting scene is that of a man facing death with proud faith in the Cause, an example to his companions because of that actual companionship – the companionship which is the greatest redeeming feature of war. For dependence on and helpful aid to others requires a cataclysm such as war to bring them about on a general scale, Man having grown cynical correspondingly with his advance from the persecution and sudden death which constantly faced his ancestors.

We resumed our advance, being soon in action again when an enemy train attacked us. Cut off from retreat by the line (running from Madrid to El Escorial via Pozuelo) being blown up behind it, the train was set on fire by petrol and bombs.[80] Following this action, we were halted a few miles out of Pozuelo, and then abruptly relieved in the advance by Moors. We marched back through Pozuelo, on to the scene of the enemy tank attack, and thence to the village of Majadahonda,[81] on which we advanced in battle formation, only to find it unoccupied by the enemy. Here we settled down, at evening time, in a shallow trench we made, to pass a bitterly cold night reminiscent of the Manzanares one, for the blankets as usual were not brought up, this time owing to enemy tanks roaming across the road leading back to Boadilla. Fortunately, I had a very thin captured cloak – carried bandolier-wise during the day – and spent a faintly passable night, although the *toreador* in my *escuadra*, similarly clad, was by the morning in need of intense resuscitation from the effects of cold during the night.

Time passed comfortably enough in these trenches, which were covered over the next day with house doors and other boards from the deserted village, and the dug-outs lined with straw. Boredom was relieved one day by the arrest and shooting of two imitation peasants who had allegedly come to this front line deserted village to sell us oranges. If they had been Spaniards it might have passed as unsuspicious, but, colossal blunder, one was a Frenchman whose accent gave him and his comrade away! We also conducted a day's operations from Majadahonda in order to assist an advance from Brunete to the westwards, doing some slight damage to the enemy, and driving their line back more on El Escorial, which could be seen away to the north. The enemy also attacked us about this time, but three tanks which were accompanying them were put on fire – two by anti-tank guns and the other by a shell from our trench mortars – and the attack fizzled out.

CHAPTER FOURTEEN
NON-PAYING TOURIST

The other thing of note which occurred while we were in this village was the near-shooting of a sergeant. It came about casually enough, and clearly demonstrated the reason for the little use of the whip at the front.[82] On sentry duty one night, I was foolish enough to let my eyes wander behind me, to where my corporal and the rest of the *escuadra* were gambling with another, similarly constituted, group of *compañeros*. The sergeant of a nearby *pelotón*, happening to pass by, spotted my lapse, although the fog was quite thick. He severely reprimanded my corporal and I, but then walked away as if the matter had been finished with. My two and a half hours of night duty shortly afterwards finished. I was relieved by a fresh sentry, and took the place he had vacated in the game. It would now be fair to state that our sobriety was not too good; although my own was perfect, as I had got onto the fire-step[83] before the liquor appeared, and until my relief had only taken a small tot. The others, however, had been busy with the brandy (sale of which, with tobacco, formed a valuable perquisite of the cooks). Suddenly, the sergeant reappeared behind us, out of the fog where he had evidently been watching; the sentry, hearing his approach, immediately whirled round and challenged him. The sergeant, obviously looking for a 'case', took advantage of this to order me to take the stand again, and led the other off to the company sergeant major (temporary commander of our section). The charges was insubordination, the sentry, under reprimand, having insisted upon his right to challenge anybody approaching at night whether from front or rear, and the sergeant's opinion being otherwise. His crime was inattention to duty – for not keeping his gaze forwards – and drunkenness, which was incontestable. Persisting in his right to challenge, the sentry got a beating-up from the CSM and was then marched back past our part of the line by the sergeant who was taking him to be put in custody in the village. As the dim figures went past in the fog, up sprang the rifles of several men taking aim at the sergeant. However, the two corporals, inspired by long years of Legion discipline, immediately kicked them in their posteriors, and took their rifles off them. In the next instant, the fog had hidden the sergeant, still unconscious of his narrow escape.

Even the corporals were sorry the next morning, when the erring sentry returned, having been beaten up by the sergeant and others during the night, although the shooting of the sergeant might have cost the lives of all. Later, having had several near shaves in action from 'enemy' bullets fired from the rear, the sergeant got a transfer to another *bandera*.

Nine days of Majadahonda saw us set off (on 19 January) on a march to the village of Villaviciosa de Odón, twelve kilometres to the south, where we arrived the same afternoon, having taken our time on the way. Two days were spent here, in which I inspected the chateau, seeing the bedroom where Charles V, I believe, died;[84] this was one of the very few Spanish castles that I saw which conformed to the heavily fortified type. Another march, this time at night, took us to the village of Fuenlabrada, a further twelve and a half kilometres southwards; and the following night we went on in the same direction to Torrejón de la Calzada, another nineteen kilometres. During the following day, we rested there but just before midnight set off again for Valdemoro, a town due south of Madrid on the Córdoba road and about ten kilometres away. It had begun pouring with rain. We marched through the town in the early morning, and out onto the Córdoba road, where we halted, with the rain still pouring down. Those who had blankets, carried as bandoliers, got some shelter under them, as I did under my cloak, but many were without any protection. Dawn came, disclosing nearby a Moorish *tabor*, artillery, tanks, etc. – obviously preparations for a large-scale attack. But the artillery was unable to leave the road, and other problems were in evidence owing to torrential all-night rain having turned the baked plain of yesterday into a morass. So about eight o'clock we returned into the town, which all this time had offered unavailing shelter just behind us.

The preparations for any advance being always of the most careful and secret nature, owing to the enormously enhanced spying possibilities in any civil war, and no prospect of us sleeping or stopping at Valdemoro having been considered in advance, there were no billets available. The town was almost fully occupied, its inhabitants having so far seen little of the war.[85] A large convent was, eventually, taken over from its caretakers – the nuns having been dispossessed by the Reds – and, along with the Moors, we at last moved out of the relentless rain.

After a few days in this billet, which Kozma and I spent making Moorish friends and attending their usual evening sing-songs, the continuing rain suspended any plans for advance, and we were marched back to Torrejón. This place consisted of a very large farmhouse and about twenty other houses; we took up billets again in the buildings of the former, as we had done on our previous stay five days before. Here – owing possibly to my previous award of *'distinguido'* – I got a step up at the beginning of February. I was promoted even above many of longer service (Kozma, for instance), being made *legionario de primera clase*, or lance-corporal, entitling me to one-halfpenny a day more pay! This was a step that I honestly considered justified. Before his transfer to our platoon, my corporal [i.e., Espí] had been company trumpeter, a position he had filled for the previous seven years. This meant a lot of extra work for me, all for nothing in terms of pay, since I was the only *veterano* in his *escuadra*. Of active service as an infantryman Espí had known nothing, and was as ignorant of tactics as of his routine duties of corporal, things which I had picked up in my three and a half months' service. I had not begrudged him this extra work as it gave me a privileged place in the *escuadra*, while he often, being a heavy gambler, passed little perquisites my way.

Several days afterwards, a further development took place when the captain of the company [Aranda Mata] asked me to become his batman. This was an offer which, on the advice of Kozma and several others, my corporal being naturally the greatest objector, I accepted. I was to occupy this position for some time. Towards the end of this period as a batman, I did become indeed sick of it, but at this time, I had only an old soldier's way of looking at a cushy job. It has been said, with some faint justification, that 'an old soldier is he who jumps in the first convenient shell-hole during an attack and stays there'; but I accepted the job from every other reason but funk, which is my only justification for accepting it.

So it was as a batman, and not as one of the PBI, that I followed the *bandera* when it left Torrejón for Valdemoro, to again commence the advance. Valdemoro was left behind us on the afternoon of 11 February, and for the night we were encamped in the open country between that town and the village of San Martín de la Vega, situated between the Córdoba and Valencia main roads, and our first objective. The next morning the *bandera* marched to the attack, and this time I was left behind with the other batmen, to guard nothing more lethal than my officer's clothes trunks![86]

Of the following account of the attempted cutting of the Valencia road it will thus be understood that it was not witnessed by me as an actual front-line soldier – except at night times, which were passed in the line – as all my previous experiences had been, but as a non-combatant. On the other hand, owing to the fact of being the company commander's batman, a privileged one for being in sole attendance when the captain held his regular nightly council of war to discuss the day's events with his officers, I was enabled to gain a far greater idea of the general situation; while my trips up and down the line enabled me to see the reinforcements, etc., coming up.

To show the importance of cutting the enemy communications along the Valencia–Madrid main road, it is necessary to state that out of Madrid run seven main roads – to Córdoba, Toledo, Portugal, Corunna, Navarre, Barcelona and Valencia respectively – and only the last remained to be cut. Once that was done, Madrid would be compelled to sue for surrender, which apart from its military value would be a crushing blow to the enemy morale. From the map [see p. 93] it will be seen that our front nearest to this road stretched from Ciempozuelos to a point north of La Marañosa, and at a distance varying from ten miles to far less. Between this line and our objective lay the villages of San Martín and Morata de Tajuña, connected by a very mediocre road running through a wild and mountainous country. The two villages were also separated by the broad width of the River Jarama, too deep to allow men to ford it, but crossed by a nice modern bridge at San Martín. It was almost certain to be blown up, and so pontoons for passing the river had been sent up with engineers.

CHAPTER FIFTEEN
THE VALENCIA ROAD[87]

On 12 February the attack began, being launched against San Martín by my *bandera*, with Moorish *tabors* on the hills on either side of us. Other *banderas*, *requetés* and Moors were tactically concerned at other parts of the front, while I believe supporting shows were also carried on in the University City, to ensure the keeping of large enemy reserves busy. With our usual formation – artillery preparation, tanks leading, with the men advancing in extended order in dashes from cover to cover, gradually drawing near enough to dominate the enemy trenches either by fire or hand-grenades – San Martín was taken before nightfall. The enemy, all members of the International Brigade, fled to a line of trenches, well-prepared on the range of hills just across the river and commanding the bridge. A night's sleep and the passage of the bridge, which the enemy by some foolish blunder

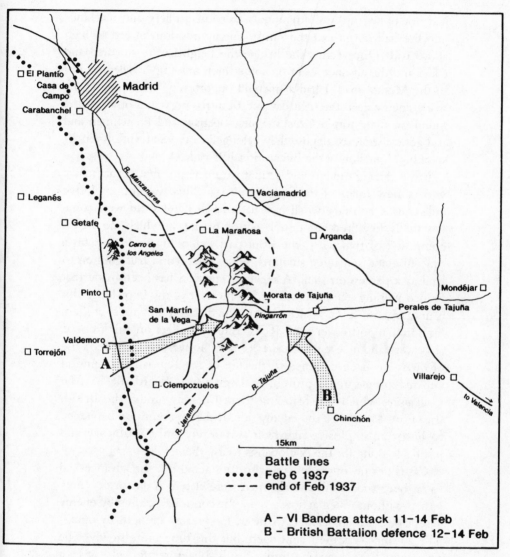

The battle of Jarama, February 1937.

had not blown up, was attempted, after our artillery and machine-gun fire had dominated the similar enemy positions placed so high above us.[88] Once across the bridge the heights were stormed and taken and the advance went on some three miles up a valley parallel to the Morata road. I had a splendid opportunity of examining the many enemy dead the next day and from passports and other papers found on them found Czechs, Poles, Belgians and Frenchmen and had good reason to suppose they belonged to the Sixteenth (French-speaking) Battalion of the International Brigade.[89]

It was during these two days that we made our first acquaintance with a new form of enemy playfulness. This was the explosive bullet, used contrary to all international principles. So were some few shells they fired of a double-action nature, in which the shell is composed of two parts, the front part exploding in the air on a time-fuse and spreading shrapnel, while the second half goes on to land as a percussion shell. A recent accusation has been made that Franco is using explosive bullets. To the best of my knowledge this is now true on some small scale, but the first and only users of them for some months were the Reds. Enemy bullets on this front at least were about seventy-five per cent explosive, while Franco's use of them has been confined to the use of the Russian ammunition and machine-guns captured, in large part, aboard the SS *Mar Cantábrico*, which was bringing them (illegally, under the British flag) from Mexico to the enemy side. If that ammunition happened to be of an explosive nature it was surely only a salutory and justifiable thing for the Nationalists to use them![90]

Casualties on our side were also substantial but the advance had so far been successful, and the men were elated. A day or two now passed without much action, except for continual strafing by enemy aeroplanes, which seemed to be in far greater strength to ours.[91] The advance was then continued, but this time more slowly. The remnants of the enemy in front of us had been reinforced – at least this was the first time we had seen them – by the Fifteenth (English-speaking) Battalion. Of course, our men were opposed by superior numbers but it must be candidly admitted, with (after all) some national pride, although I still consider their cause a false one, that the latter presented us with more solid opposition than we were accustomed to. It was composed of many ex-servicemen, and led by many British ex-officers (papers found on one dead officer stated ex-Royal Scots). Once, in particular, they made a bayonet charge against us at dusk. The only one I had previously seen, in my first action, was made by us against the Navalcarnero trenches, mainly by seasoned African veterans who had often used bayonets against the Moors. Most of these seasoned *Legionarios* had since passed on to even warmer climes, and those recruited in their places had had no bayonet exercise at all, not even against the traditional sandbag target. So, momentarily the *bandera* gave ground, only to recover and magnificently drive them back. I was fortunately on the scene to see it, but being armed only with the captain's lunch basket, gave quite as much ground as any![92]

Serge Tchige, the White Russian of the Twenty-First, previously mentioned as a companion of Kozma and I, acted with great courage here. He stayed put, forming a rallying point, even though his company had been the first of the *bandera* to give and had given the most ground. But his action went unrecognized, even by promotion; he remained only a second-class *Legionario* (albeit an ex-officer of the Czarist Navy and also of Wrangel's Army).[93] As for Kozma, he was not present at this time, having been wounded on the sixteenth by an explosive bullet in the right groin – indubitably fired by a member of the British Battalion – from which wound he died in hospital on 9 March. This was a great loss to me as a more pleasant comrade and better gentleman would be hard to find. I had last seen him in the valley above San Martín, when he seemed 'fey'; his last words to me being that he was perfectly at peace and prepared to meet his end, a state of mind from which I had been unable to move him.[94]

The move in which Kozma was downed brought us to the Pingarrón Hill, the sides of which were covered with olive groves, making it impossible to effect a regular defence line. We were subject to sniping from every angle, my old corporal being killed through his daily insistence on shaving – the personal deprivation here will be realized, since water had to be brought up miles, from San Martín, and then rationed out for drinking purposes only. Pierre, the young Frenchman of my Talavera recruit days, was also killed here, as were many others of the small group of foreigners in the *bandera*.

I spent the daylight hours in San Martín, only disturbed by the constant shelling of the bridge and village by enemy artillery. Proceedings were also enlivened by air battles which were sometimes staged over the village. The novelty of watching planes dashing to destruction had long worn off, but two vivid memories remain here. One the machine-gunning of a helpless pilot swinging on his parachute by the merciless victors; and the other, one of our aeroplanes which hurtled down on fire during a dog-fight involving about twenty planes, suddenly rearing up to loop before continuing its fall to destruction.

One day the officer's cook and I made a hurried trip to the town of Illescas for provisions, intending to be back in time to go up to the lines that night as usual. However, my companion's brother living in a nearby village, we decided to pay a quick visit. The cook not having seen his brother for some years, it took longer than we had thought possible to say goodbye to him – the *vino* and the local beauties being good – and it was twenty-four hours after we planned before we saw the captain again. We gave a sad (and unbelieved) recital of the hardships we had undergone while 'lost, looking for eggs'. The fact that Aranda and the other officers had had to put up with rough fare the previous night and the whole day, might have been expected to have made some disarrangement to his liver, but I got the benefit of the doubt, as a foreigner traditionally unable to understand Spanish. By the way, I can recommend the efficacy of anyone under foreign control learning as his first phrase the native equivalent of 'I do not understand'. Use of it when faced with some unpleasant task will often oblige the sending of some unfortunate native to do it, in order to avoid the tedious (and if he is wise, long) explanations otherwise needed!

One task, however, I could not escape. In San Martín one day I was requested to act as interpreter to seven English prisoners before they were sent back beyond the battle area. I found that five of them were Scotsmen, one a Londoner, and the seventh a Canadian. One claimed to be the son of an Edinburgh clergyman, but the others were ordinary workmen, much the same as those who can be seen at the local Saturday afternoon football match. They claimed to have come out to Spain to get the soft jobs they had been told they could have as ambulance drivers, or some other non-combatant work. Given weekend tickets to France and a sum of money, they had arrived in Spain via Perpignan (the International Brigade centre in France). They found themselves without option but to join the Brigade, and had been sent to Albacete for training – which I knew to be true from a 'daily order' I had found up the line. They said this was the first time they themselves had been in the line. They admitted that Brigade losses had been heavy, a fact we also knew from the constant stream of deserters, mainly French, who came over, and that, of the Anglo-American Battalion's commencing strength of 650 men, only 200 remained, a statement partly confirmed later by the British Communist Party in a bulletin giving their dead as 100 and 300 wounded. One thing worth noting were the new Russian rifles with which they were armed, while their thick khaki uniforms showed us up; their fine khaki greatcoats were especially sought after.[95]

Our own losses were about equal, and of the *escuadra* I had belonged to at the beginning of the month only one man remained. Accordingly, after one last and unavailing attack against the enemy lines just above Morata, my *bandera* was withdrawn from the Jarama front on the 22nd of the month. To its credit were another ten days of hard fighting, a successful advance of some six miles, and another decimation of the ranks, for which it again received the *Medalla Militar*, with my company also getting yet another such gong for itself.

CHAPTER SIXTEEN
EL PLANTIO

As the attack was still going on, we only moved a few miles away, to the village of Pinto, near which we stopped for four days with German artillery – mere guards, and not shock-troops any longer.[96] We had done our best and our lines were so near the Valencia road that our artillery could keep up some sort of blockade, if not an effective one, especially at night, on it. Then, at length, a collection of lorries and omnibuses came for us and off we went, once more a noisy mob of tourists, up through Leganés, Móstoles, Boadilla del Monte, and finally found ourselves relieving Moors at El Plantío on the main Madrid–Corunna highway.

El Plantío was a deserted village, about ten kilometres from, and with a good view of, Madrid. It constituted an example of the ribbon building so decried by road-safety experts. In the large house selected as a residence by the *Plana Mayor* (HQ) of the *bandera*, the Count de López-Muñoz, a former Spanish ambassador to Portugal, had lived. This example is typical of the type of people who had lived in El Plantío in more peaceful days. Between us and Aravaca (to the south-east and also in our hands) the main road was impassable, owing to its thorough lack of shelter, while further on lay Pozuelo and Madrid. A little distance away from us to the north-west was the village of Las Rozas, the northern end of the Nationalist line, with further on still, El Escorial and the Sierra de Guadarrama. To the west lay Boadilla and Majadahonda, separated from us by several miles of thick woods, in the centre of which was the big Casa Oriol, half palace and half country mansion. This place, with its private chapel and enormous stables, was reputedly the property of the Count de Romanones, favourite of ex-King Alfonso, and the owner of property in many parts of Spain. On the north-east side of the road and about a hundred yards from it, El Plantío was bounded on the east side by a high wall with wooded land beyond it running as far as the eye could see – probably the hunting park of El Pardo.[97] The wall, honeycombed with loopholes, was our front line, and the enemy were in some unseen position about half a mile away in the woods. Here, under the protecting shelter of the wall we settled down, the company in dug-outs, the officers in suitable and convenient houses.

The night we arrived and after we had settled down, firing broke out from the Moorish positions on our immediate left. Our sentries firing warning shots also, the whole line broke into life, a party to which the enemy contributed with mortar shells. The firing slackening off, we could make out the cries of the genial *'paísos'* – the familiar noun for Moors – bidding us greeting. It was the same *tabor* with which we had advanced into the University City in the previous November, and hauling us out of our beds in this manner was their humorous way of expressing their appreciation of our renewed acquaintance! At least we had the consolation of knowing that the enemy had also been awakened to repel our 'attack'. These Moorish night 'attacks' are very frequent and are typical of that peculiar humour they possess. I have seen the *bandera* roused at night on many different fronts by the same thing, as when they start heavy firing the 'stand to' order must be given in case it is a real enemy attack. It undoubtedly must harass the nerves of the enemy, but it was also disconcerting, to say the least, to us. Some day the Moors will cry wolf once too often and let themselves in for severe trouble.

Several genuine night attacks, supported by tanks, did take place however, but although the wood gave the enemy good shelter, a narrow clearing between the wood and the wall had been laid with barbed-wire and the chances against a stray bullet coming through a loophole at night time being very high, we remained secure behind our thick protector. I think it is highly improbable that any advance will be attempted by the Nationalists on this sector until the forces south of Madrid, at least, have considerably advanced eastwards, as with only a light holding force, the yard-thick wall provides an almost impregnable line against the enemy. Its only vulnerability is to landmines, but these would need to be launched from a considerable distance away, and against even this contingency precautions have been taken which would probably be effective.

Here in this idyllic spot we settled down to await the recruits we so badly needed to bring us back up to fighting strength. They kept coming in, but only in groups of two dozen or so, and at irregular intervals. Continued operations against the Valencia road necessitated most fresh men being sent there instead, from the depots in Talavera. Many new faces were natives of the Balearic Islands, whom we mistrusted to some extent, partly through their relationship to the Communist Catalans, but mostly from an unhappy event occasioned by three of them.

Some fifty yards in front of the wall, a small earthwork had been dug, its position on the crown of a small, cleared hill commanding a clear view of any attacking force. To this position a corporal and his *escuadra* were sent, in rota, every morning at dawn, to be withdrawn at dusk. A short distance behind the wall, close to the villa which housed the *Plana Mayor*, stood a high brick tower of some description, on which a sentry was permanently stationed, with good sight of both the earthwork and an enemy outpost another fifty yards further out. A Spanish corporal named González, with many years Legion service and some five or more wound stripes, returning from hospital in charge of one batch of recruits, was given an *escuadra* formed from one *veterano* and three of these *'quintos'*. One day, he left for the earthwork with his squad, and the sentry on the tower duly noted their safe arrival. Not very long afterwards, the latter's gaze swinging round onto the outpost, he was in time to see the disarmed corporal and *veterano* being forced by the three *quintos* at rifle-point into the enemy post. It was too late to do anything except sound the alarm, since it was not safe to approach the now-deserted outpost until dusk, when an officer accompanied by several men went out, to return later with confirmation of the disaster. It had evidently been done by surprise as no shot had been heard, neither was there any blood to be found in the earthwork. Naturally this affair brought discredit on many of the other *quintos* - especially when another one was shot for shouting Anarchist slogans when in liquor. After these incidents, the older members of the *bandera* looked upon the newer very warily, as they had no desire to emulate the unfortunate González, whom death had certainly claimed, since his long service and wound stripes would have weighed the scales against him.[98]

At the beginning of March, the news of the Italian defeat at Guadalajara seeped through to us, helped by enemy propagandists. It caused not the despair that the latter hoped for but ironic 'I told you so' comments upon the Italian morale. The Italians have had the name of 'Seville soldiers' tagged on them from the long time they remained inactive in that city, whispers which had been driven underground by their capture of Málaga; but the hurried and demoralized retreat of this mechanized column, reminiscent of what we were used to seeing the enemy militia do, brought them raging forth anew. Besides, we being infantry of the old type, there was a great deal of 'them there new-fangled ways' and 'you can't beat the PBI' attitude about our remarks. Being friendly with several Germans in a nearby tank corps, I had heard the news about Guadalajara quickly, and the Germans were, paradoxically since they are Italian allies, as pleased as we were to hear of the retreat. It was a striking example of the collapse of morale in regular troops, occasioned by the International Brigade, enemy air strafing and the counter-opposition of Russian tanks — boasted of by the Moscow newpaper *Izvestia* in ways we were accustomed to. But the tragi-comic thing was the distance in reverse covered by the Italians, before Moorish and Legionary troops got among them to stop the rot.

The days passed, often only enlivened by the sound and sometimes sight of falling shells in Madrid, while we were subject to occasional bombardments from enemy mortars. The latter were punctuated with occasional propaganda leaflets, fired by a special 'gun' to add emphasis to their delivery, but as these were exhortations to murder our officers and desert, with strong protestations of their friendship to us, they seemed out of place to us mixed as they were with 'friendly' mortar shells! The propaganda game became highly developed at this time opposite us, and every night we were subjected to loudspeaker dissertations, which we often drowned by singing Legion songs and shouting studied insults at various governmental characters – notably the woman politician, *'La Pasionaria'*. Our playful efforts invariably produced an enemy 'close down' of their broadcasting and a renewed resorting to their mortars.

Another thing which helped to keep up our spirits was the enemy's unavailing offer to Britain and France of Spanish Morocco in exchange for active intervention – an inexcusable treachery to the Spanish people, one which Franco has also been accused of conmmitting but which, if he has, has not been so openly carried out. The other notable event to me in March was my birthday, which I turned into a fiesta by ten shillings' worth of muscatel brandy, cigars, pastries and caramels brought by a friend from Toledo – a dreadful piece of extravagance, representing eight days' pay. This day was a curious one, illustrative of Nature's fickle moods. The morning's sun rose caressingly over the roof tops of Madrid and the birds commenced their whistling in the pine forest behind us. Not a shot breaking the stillness it all seemed like a picnic, yet the enemy were only half a mile away, and the siege guns giving their morning greetings to the beleaguered capital soon dispelled the illusion. Midday saw a freak hailstorm which only lasted five minutes but upset the weather to such an extent that in the afternoon came heavy rain to be followed by cold winds and an early dusk. It only wanted thunder and lightning to have displayed the attributes of twelve months in twelve hours.

CHAPTER SEVENTEEN
A CORPORAL AT EASE

On the night of 8 April, we were all pulled out of bed by a falling curtain of enemy trench mortar shells. It seemed as if we were being attacked in force, an assumption strengthed by enemy tanks which, hidden by the thick wood, also began shelling us. The whole of the skyline to the south-east, and even as far south as Carabanchel, was lit up by shell explosions, the University City being as perfectly visible as it usually was in daylight, while some firing was also taking place at Las Rozas to the north of us. It was apparent to our own immediate perception that a general attack was commencing on a twelve-mile front – and for all we knew it may have been going on all the way southwards to the Jarama. However, the activity opposite us and towards Las Rozas died down after an hour or two, and it became obvious that it had only been a feint to keep any immediate reserves we had behind us in a quandary. But the terrific noise to the south, from Aravaca to Carabanchel, persisted, and in the stillness now fallen over our sector we could even make out the crackle of rapid infantry fire.

Several days later, the attack having been still carried on day and night, yet our sector being still quiet, my company was detailed to act separately from the *bandera*, in Aravaca (closer to Madrid on our right) where the remnants of the Fourth *Bandera* were still holding on. Although it was only a few miles away from us along the main road, this route was impassable, being under enemy fire, and the journey involved a roundabout journey, via Boadilla and Pozuelo to the rear, of at least ten miles. At Aravaca, we took up positions reinforcing the Fourth. For their magnificent example of holding on in the face of outnumbering masses of Russians, Germans and Czechs of the International Brigade, and the terrific tank attacks, in which the latter often came nearly to their wire defences, the Fourth were to be awarded the highest military decoration of Spain, the Grand Laureated Cross of San Ferdinand.[99] For our part, we found ourselves faced across the plain by a dreadful carnage of piles and piles of enemy bodies. With their usual tactics, the enemy had attacked in mass formation in the face of tremendous fire. It seemed strange that such an archaic principle, demonstrated as suicidally wasteful twenty years previously, should still persist. Evidently the Russian Bear, with his usual mentality, envisaged the 'old steamroller' in its glory of the musket days. Our own methods of attack, previously enunciated, bore fair chance of success and with comparatively light casualties, but, given brave defenders, these enemy tactics could not succeed until all our machine-gunners, at least, had been wiped out.

A day's work at Aravaca, another inside the University City five miles away, then we got back to El Plantío, the enemy offensive having already begun to fizzle out. Aided by aviation, artillery, tanks, and in the Casa del Campo, armoured trains, it had had for its objectives the easing of our operations against Bilbao, and the breaking of our communications with the University City, which lie through a long deep trench, subject at intervals to attacks, of which this latest one was by far the most determined ever launched. Naturally, its own weight gave it a slight, but very slight, gain of ground, mainly in Carabanchel Bajo, but the lifeline remained unimpaired, and for all the enemy's heavy casualties (and ours) the advantage they gained was negligible.

On the sixteenth of the month [i.e., April], a day or so after our return to El Plantío, I got rid of my non-combatant shackles and settled down in a dug-out – at last with a squad of my own. I had been promoted *cabo* (corporal), an appointment officially confirmed a few days later. It meant a daily wage of 1.5 pesetas (one shilling and sixpence). The same day, a truce was agreed upon by the two sides in which to bury the hundreds of dead now piled up in the Casa de Campo area – the Nationalists claimed that the government forces had left 2,800 men on the field – and soon burial parties of both sides were scouring the battlefield. On the same day also, far away to the south in Córdoba province, the entry of the Valencia Government forces into the monastery-fortress of the Virgén de la Cabeza was announced. Behind thick ramparts twelve hundred Nationalists and their families had fought since the beginning of the civil war. They had resisted land and air assaults for nine months, which was an even greater feat than the (more successful) defence of the Alcázar of Toledo. The Government forces have a way, for them unfortunate, of spoiling the propaganda value of success, in this case by the slaughter of the defenders. In response, our well-directed pointers towards the little military value of the place helped to maintain the glitter of our successful defence of the Casa de Campo.[100]

Towards the end of the month we were taken in lorries to the village of Villanueva de la Cañada, directly to the south of El Escorial.[101] We had been at El Plantío for two months, but were still under strength, as the Jarama and Guadalajara operations, and the latest diversionary offensives, had swallowed up most of the recruits before they got as far as us. All the same, Villanueva was a pleasant little village, hardly touched by the war. Only a few hundred yards to the rear of the forward line, we took over from a whole battalion of regular troops from the Canary Islands. How were the mighty fallen – the victorious Sixth occupying positions which the lowly *'pipis'* (as the conscripts are known) had been thought good enough to hold! In itself that is an insight into the low strength of the *bandera*. The trenches were on the rim of high ground, and on the side of similar hilly ground across the valley, in front of us and about one and a half miles away, were the enemy trenches. Behind these, to the north and across another valley, rose the towering snow-capped Guadarramas. In this second and larger valley lay the world-renowned El Escorial, still in enemy hands, although a part of its direct road to the capital lay in our hands, from Las Rozas to Aravaca. So quiet was the front here that we used to go down to the valley in front of our lines to wash ourselves and our clothes, while a local farmer, with the indifference to politics general to his class, ploughed his nearby field unconcernedly.

The only shots which disturbed the silence were those fired through inexperience by recruits, who now, suddenly, came to us in two large batches. With *vino* and other luxuries obtainable in quantity from the village, life seemed very pleasant. The villagers, too, must have been happy, owing to the far greater pay we got than the regulars who had been there previously. My own *escuadra* consisted of five Spaniards, one a lance-corporal, and my only duties were now three and a half hours surveillance of the sentries of my section each night, while my days were free. This meant sundry hours stolen in the village, mostly in the company of the white Russian ex-naval officer of the Twenty-First, previously mentioned, [i.e., Serge Tighe] and a German corporal of the machine-gun company, Karl Knoll, a veteran with seven years' Legion service. Of all the bibulous men in the Legion and, believe me, their name is also legion, Karl must have been one of the worst. In Villanueva he was perfectly content, possessing such a persuasive manner that he could get credit where even an officer would have been refused, and thus got all the drink that even his wine tun of a stomach required. Habits such as his would have often resulted in loss of stripes, if Karl had not been so dependable that, whether he was drunk or sober, his gun had always been to the fore in repelling attacks. During marches, even though he might be full to capacity with booze, his huge frame carried the heavy Hotchkiss gun with ease and without lagging behind.

It was customary to serve out brandy to the troops occasionally, especially during the cold nights of this time of the year; one bottle for each *pelotón*, so that it meant a third of a bottle for each *escuadra* – hardly more than a tot for each man. One night in this place, Serge's *escuadra* got the bottle first and it was left two thirds full, ready to be passed on to the other recipients next morning. The effect of his tot soon wearing off, Serge (who was on sentry duty) felt cold and determined to have the tiniest sip from the now-forbidden bottle – but no more. His 'sip' ended in the whole lot disappearing. Next morning, to the execrations of the luckless two squads and the huge merriment of the rest of the *bandera*, Serge was hauled before his captain and given seven days in hard labour.

This is done as part of a punishment squad in which the *bandera* places its bad boys for varying periods, though if we go into action they are released for combat irrespective the time left to serve, which is then cancelled. A tough soldier, attached to *Bandera* HQ, has permanent charge of this gang, although sometimes he is left without 'clients'. Under his sole authority, from which there is no appeal (the prisoner's rank notwithstanding), their time is worked out. Usually, if in billets, they are used as scavengers or beasts of burden, and the shaven-headed drones must obey the *pelotonero*'s orders, no matter how senseless they are. At Torrejón I had seen some unfortunates cleaning the roads of mule manure using their bare hands as shovels – although this was exceptional. As their overseer is not sparing with the physical punishment he gives them for the slightest offence, men often come out in worse shape than at their entry. But the aim of this *'pelotón'* is the enforcement of a dread of more punishment, and a determination to steer clear of its clutches for the future, and here it rarely fails, except with habitual drunkards.

My own *escuadra* gave me little trouble, though its members were with only one exception much older than I was.[102] It indeed did its best for me, as at one parade when we turned out for a lieutenant-colonel in Villanueva, I was commended for their smart appearance – no bad thing at a time when both 'spit and polish' were at a premium. I was glad of this success, owing to the envy which my promotions over their heads (both to lance and full corporal) had caused to some few others. However, one bright spark in my squad, a farm labourer before enlistment, did occasion me some worry at the beginning by his excessive drinking. Now, I would be the last to object to drinking when off duty, but this man disappeared one morning to the village and returned in a drunken state at dusk. He had missed his share of day duty, and was now incapable of doing his night sentry shift as well, so that his comrades had to share his work out between them for twenty-four hours. Having no wish to place him in the punishment squad, I put him on duty as soon as the next day dawned to do his missed shares of duty – about six consecutive hours in all – which kept him busy until midday. But the sergeant of our platoon coming along and finding from him the reason for his prolonged duty, immediately gave him enough work to do until dusk, digging useless trenches. All this conspired to keep him sober for a short period, and thereafter he took good care not to filch his comrades' rest periods, but it failed to make a permanent impression. That was all I could hope for, as the Legion is no place for a proselytizing teetotaller.

CHAPTER EIGHTEEN

THE DEFENCE OF TOLEDO (i)

Towards the end of our stay in Villanueva, the authorities had begun to suspect an attack was being planned by the enemy from El Escorial and as a result we were kept busy strengthening, and adding to the barbed-wire defences which lay on the slope below us. One deep gully which flanked our position ran back from the valley well behind us to the left, and was particularly watched at night; but owing to lack of sufficient force it was impossible to entrench it. It is very seldom that an extended line of trenches runs for any considerable distance on either side owing to lack of men to man them, a state of things which is exploited by the Nationalists to make flanking attacks in extended order, thus reducing their casualties, but the Government side still pin their faith mostly to frontal attacks in mass formation. Their attack on this front a few months afterwards, however, took advantage of this gully, thus causing a withdrawal of the Nationalist lines to Brunete, two miles away. But my *bandera* was well away from the scene (at Segovia) by that time.

The 7 May saw the arrival of lorry-loads of Falangists of Seville. It seemed as if we were to make an attack on El Escorial while the Falangists would remain behind in Villanueva to act their usual role of rearguard. No move being made by the Falangists to relieve us from the trenches, it seemed to confirm our impression. Furthermore, a riotous joint fiesta took place in the village that night – although the Legion as a rule is unfriendly (to say the least) to the Falange. Another fact, lovingly recalled by Dame Rumour, was that we had enjoyed the rare treat of having the Legion band as our guests for the past two days. Our only previous view of them at the front had been at Navalcarnero on the last day before the main advance on the University City, although we had seen them later at Talavera, which was their depot.[103] Further comment came when the *comandante* of the *bandera* was seen to be busily engaged with an artillery officer in surveying the enemy positions; the artillery later fired a few shells at various points of the enemy positions, as if plotting ranges. One other warlike instruction had been the recent order that we were in no circumstances to be without our gas-masks. This was certainly necessary, as through lack of use of gas, we had rather contemptuously come to regard them as a superfluous piece of equipment, only to be thought of when moving on, in order not to be charged with losing official property and incurring the ensuing fine and punishment.

It was no surprise when next morning blankets were rolled up and piled aboard the lorries, and we marched out along the road to Brunete after having been at last relieved by the Falange. On the plaza at Brunete, Italian army transport lorries were waiting for us, and in we squeezed, setting off almost immediately southwards again, to Navalcarnero. It had been six months since I had seen this village and the change in it was remarkable. Hardly a trace of the near-havoc remained, houses had been reconditioned, shops were open again and the streets were crowded with civilians, both male and female, and the Falange. Particularly busy was the plaza, which had once re-echoed to the Legion songs; of those singers, hardly thirty now remained in my company, the majority of whom were now sergeants and corporals, while we did not have one officer left with us who had marched with the company in those days. The captain and *Alférez* Blanco (who was then my section commander) were the only two left alive, and they had now left us; the captain, promoted *comandante*, for Morocco, and the *alférez*, promoted *teniente*, to *bandera* adjutant. All the present company officers were entirely new. The new captain had only been with us a week, while the four others only joined us at El Plantío in March, and knew nothing of the Legion, three of them being lowly *'pipis'* and the other a Falangist – which accounted a lot for what was soon to follow.

The lorries took the west-bound road out of Navalcarnero, a route immediately seized upon as proof that we were off to make a flanking attack on El Escorial, but to the amazement of the knowledgeable ones we were suddenly switched off down a road leading south, and thus soon driving further and further away from El Escorial. We shortly arrived at a lovely village, which we knew could not be very far from Toledo, and it is a curious fact that of all the villages I was in, the name of this one is the only one that eludes me. Here, the old agricultural life of Spain was going on in its old way, medieval in its ancientness, as for example, wooden ploughs – as if the inhabitants were hundreds of miles, and not just twenty from the war scenes. The little taverns were soon full to overflowing, and we felt fully recompensed for having lost the prospects of another 'scrap' – at which sentiments the God of War must have rocked on his throne with laughter, holding as he was the bombshell which was soon to destroy us.

Contrary to custom, there was no roll-call at eight that night and it was very late when the noise in the village subsided and the last rowdy sought his bed. Next day was again spent by the troops lounging about, though I, and consequently my squad, spent the day in the billets, seeing that they were kept clean and the equipment not stolen. At eight o'clock, the sergeants appeared, and I had to call the parade for roll-call. This being naturally unexpected, the majority were in the taverns, necessitating the formation of patrols to round them up. Roll-call over, we settled down on the floors to sleep, but almost immediately had to spring up to attention at the announcement by the sentry of our officer's arrival. Came the order to fall in, in full marching kit, with blankets slung bandolier-fashion around each man.

The stillness of the night was soon shattered by the arrival of omnibuses of all descriptions, big and little, good and bad – the Italian transports had left us upon arrival in the village – and we were soon piling into them, off the Devil knew where, but although the Legion is his foster child he neglected this time to take us into his confidence. Through the darkness we sped, not recognizing a thing, until at last we started passing houses, beyond which those of us who had once been stationed in Toledo recognized the billets we

110

had then occupied, the Escuela de los Maestros. We had evidently been brought to Toledo – but why so hurriedly in the middle of the night? The buses went on past the college, taking the fine promenade which lies to the west of the city, crossing the Rio Tajo (Tagus) by the ancient Puente de San Martín, defended at either end by the battlemented towers through which the road passed, the buses passing through them by the proverbial hair's breadth. The road, now climbing upwards at a steep angle, opened up before us again, until we came to a sudden halt. We got down to the ground and, stiff with lack of movement in the overcrowded vehicles, marched off the side of the road into an olive grove under the trees, in which, *escuadra* by *escuadra*, we settled down. The buses having moved off, only the sound of intermittent firing nearby disturbed the quietness of the olive grove. At first this meant to us nothing more than that we were near the front line. The halt at the unknown village had been taken to portend a course of instructions, which the *quintos* were sadly in need of; even the move to Toledo had been guessed to be for this purpose. But developments soon revealed that we were to be reinforcements. It was certain that it was under the most extraordinary circumstances as, if we were to relieve any troops, the buses would have been kept waiting to take the latter away. With the puzzle unsolved, and under the gaze of myriads of stars – several groups of which had rapidly become known as 'the Englishman's saucepan' – we lay down to sleep.[104]

Dawn on 10 May, and we found ourselves in a valley surrounded by high peaks. Beyond them in a southerly direction, rifle and machine-gun firing had become heavier and more regular, and now the explosions of bombs from enemy aeroplanes buzzing overhead, and artillery shells, could be heard. At last, led by the machine-gun company, we moved towards the sound of the firing, up through the olive groves, across a country road, through continued olive groves, to where a wall separated them from the uncultivated and wild heights above. Scaling the steep slopes by untrodden paths, at last we came to rest in a large grassy valley, set high up in the range of mountains with far below us the River Tajo and Toledo, the latter showing up in relief with its narrow streets and multitude of churches.[105] By the redness of its colour, the slightly undulating plain, sprinkled with orchards and farms, gave to the age-old 'city of riches' the appearance of an island washed by a sea of blood. Through a gap to the south could be seen range upon range of *sierras* running away into the purple distance – *sierras*, moreover, which though sun-kissed and pleasant to behold, held for us the ever-present menace which the enemy lands hold.

I think it was at that moment that I first realized the age-old idiocy which is war; something radiating from those beautiful peaks conveying more to me than all the wrecked homes and lives I had seen; something of the horror of fratricide which civil war wreaks, something possible of realization and yet something of that nationalism for which both sides are fighting – the one for age-old traditions, faith and culture, the other for an as yet unachieved equitable utopia. Yet evolutionary progress is and always has been achieved by unpeaceful ways and, whatever the final outcome of this present war, the mighty clash of these two opposing cultures will bear a great part in the ultimate moulding of the future Spain.

CHAPTER NINETEEN

THE DEFENCE OF TOLEDO (ii)

Over the hill top to the front of us, on which the enemy shells were continually thudding, the machine-gun company had now disappeared to assist whoever was there. The rest of us stayed in the valley. Dinner soon came up, but hardly had we finished eating, than Moorish *'mehalla'* began falling back upon us, first in couples and then in larger groups, all heading for Toledo.[106] Matters were evidently serious, so my company and the Twenty-First were taken up the hill at the double – the Twenty-Second being left in reserve in the valley. On the other

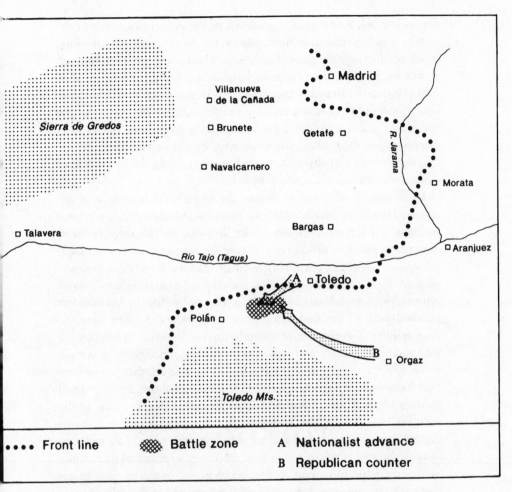

•••• Front line **▨ Battle zone** **A Nationalist advance**

B Republican counter

The action near Toledo, May 1937.

side of the hill, a wide gully ran down to the plain below us, and my section was left here as a guard against the enemy making a flanking attack up it, which they could have easily done, olive-trees reaching up almost to the top. Here we stayed, while the firing, which had died down during the retreat of the *mehalla*, revived in intensity. A short half hour, then the section was called upon to reinforce the rest of of the company up ahead. To do so involved crossing an exposed hill-top and descending another valley, where we were caught by enemy fire which cost me the first casualty of my squad, finally gaining the protection of a hedgerow on top of the slope the other side.

From here it was at last possible for us to see what we were up against. Battalions, mainly Russian, of the International Brigade were attacking our hill-top from three sides. In front, and sheltered by more olive groves, lay twenty-odd heavy tanks, pelting away at us with shells from their automatic guns, and aided by artillery, trench mortars, and aviation. Evidently a 'do or die' attack directed against Toledo, two or three miles away and only hidden from the enemy view by less than five hundred yards of the undulating ground behind us. Against them we were holding a single line of recently captured enemy trench, only a yard wide, breast-high, and made up of two unconnected lengths, each about fifty yards long and at right angles to one another. Moreover, their barbed-wire defences, being erected to keep us out, now stretched uselessly behind them. A similar but longer line of trenches away to the right was occupied by the Twenty-First, who at this moment, reduced through casualties by about half (as were our own) began running back towards the shelter of the little valley where my section had been lying. Seeing them go, our men in the trenches in front of us also began coming back, but enemy bombs and the revolvers of the officers soon returned them to a dutiable state of mind, and back they went, in time to prevent the enemy occupying the trenches.

My section went with them, and jumping down in the shallow pits we found they had become even shallower, crammed as they were with the bodies of comrades. Some were lying peacefully, killed outright by bullets, even though some of them were of the explosive type. Others were lumps of torn and mangled flesh, with arms, heads and legs littering the trench, a tribute to the marksmanship of enemy tanks and artillery. On top of this grisly mess we stood, respect for the dead forgotten in respect for life itself, and soon our rifles were pouring out destruction at the advancing hordes in mass formation below us. Advancing, wavering, retreating, advancing again – there seemed to be everlasting waves of them, until one felt as if the very dead themselves were rising to advance with them, and I realized why even the glorious Sixth with its traditions of victories won and battles lost, both with unwavering steadfastness, had succumbed to the poison of retreat. Most of it was now composed of untrained recruits averaging twenty years of age, seeing action for the first time, and without the knowledge of previous victories and many attacks repulsed to aid and consolidate them. Around this time, although I did not know of it for days afterwards, Serge Tchige was struck full in the chest by an enemy shell, grim irony of fate, fired by a Red Russian tank, the resultant explosion bespattering the ground with portions of the upper part of his body. He was a gallant gentleman and fine comrade, and it was some consolation to me that, unlike that of Kozma, his death had been painless and instantaneous. For while life is sweet so can death be, and is it not sometimes better than to live as a hideous travesty without sight, without one or all of one's members?

We stood our ground in the two lines of trenches, in front of and slightly above the hedge previously mentioned, though new casualties were constantly being sustained. Shortly, only one sergeant was left with us, belonging to my own platoon, named Matilla, a fine *Legionario* of the old type with little to say and lots of energy. The trench sticking out at right angles to ours was empty of defenders except for two gallant foreigners, a Frenchman and a German. Queer how two national types separated by centuries of war and mutual dislike were friendly allies in defence of another nation – but of such is the Legion. I had, of my own initiative, sent a man back to the hedge for ammunition, supplies of which were being used up rapidly. His movement almost started another retreat, so nervy had those unfortunate *quintos* become. After consultation with Matilla, it was decided that I should go out to that almost deserted trench. Calling some half-dozen men to follow me – hardly one of my own squad remained – I got across the barbed-wire fence and into the trench, to find that only two Portuguese had actually come with me. With only a light machine-gun, Browning type, and a few clips of ammunition, their action was indeed commendable, and it is to be regretted that a shell landing on top of them soon killed them, as they had shown up the Spaniards whose land we were defending. Indeed, this whole time, the position had been occupied only by foreigners, of French, German, Portuguese and British nationality, yet it was an extremely important one offering as it did an opportunity of enfilading the advancing Russians.

After the Portuguese, the German was the next to go, wounded in the chest, and the Frenchman, after lasting another half hour was struck sideways through the mouth, the bullet smashing several teeth. For a short period I was alone in the trench, getting my ammunition, bullet by bullet, out of the boxes of machine-gun cartridges which lay about. By now my own rifle had been smashed and torn from my grasp by a bullet, so I plundered another from the plentiful supply. By now, the machine-gunners had been almost wiped out, since their Hotchkiss weapons were too long to be fitted inside the trench and they had been mounted on top, thus exposing the gunners to terrific casualties. Even those of them that had the captured Russian-type Maxims were similarly exposed; indeed there was not a single machine-gun actively supporting the whole company at this point. At last the Twenty-Second was brought up from reserve and filtered in to our lines. I was no longer so lonely, and as the sun was beginning to set, it seemed as if the falling night would give us shelter. A bullet now struck me under the right nostril, coming out again just below the ear and, momentarily, I was literally knocked off my feet. The blood pouring down and feeling as if my whole head had been blown off I picked myself up and lifted myself out of the trench in order to pass backwards for treatment. I had to get through that barbed wire behind us, and was just about to clear the last strands when another bullet – as previously explained they were coming from all angles – took me under the right kneecap, coming out in the muscle of my calf. My legs collapsing under me, I somersaulted through the remaining barbed-wire. Here, only fifty yards from the hedge behind which the officers and some aides were sheltering, calls for aid being unavailing, I commenced a crawl which seemed more like fifty miles, amid the hum of bullets fired at my scrambling frame. Two Spaniards did, at the last, rush out to drag me the few remaining yards into shelter. A hurried bandaging was followed by an agonizing journey on the pack-saddle of an ammunition mule, down through the darkness which had now set in. On the road far below, ambulances made from converted omnibuses were waiting, and off we went to hospital. It was an unpleasant journey, rendered more so by the rutted road and (I suspect) greaseless springs of the 'ambulance'. But my day's work was done.[107]

It later emerged that during this fight our artillery had been hopelessly bombarding areas way behind the actual enemy lines, and as a result the commanding officer and several of his staff were suspended, and, after later court-martial, shot. Reduced to only a quarter of its previous strength, the Sixth *Bandera* was relieved of its labours the day after my injury. Eventually we were given the Grand Laureated Cross of San Ferdinand for our contribution. Three other Legionary *banderas*, the Fourth, Eighth and Twelfth, were also involved in the engagement, before enemy attacks finally subsided on the Toledo front.

CHAPTER TWENTY

EXIT

We were soon in a hospital at Toledo, where I met Karl Knoll who had been wounded in the stomach, and where everyone was full of anxious fear that the Reds might break through. I wonder how many of those nurses and civilians of all ages who tended us survived the bombs dropped on the hospital a few days later by enemy aeroplanes? Here we stayed only a few hours before being sent on to Griñón. This had at one time been a convent school, from which both the nuns and the children had long since been driven out by a marauding band of Reds, and on our conquest of the territory converted into a hospital, for which, with its long dormitories and classrooms, it was admirably suited. A week's stay here, and I was transferred to the military hospital of San Domingo at Talavera, an excellent young creature soothing my troubles away for another nine days until, still a bed patient, I was sent to Cáceres, an old town of Roman origin near the Portuguese frontier.

It was in one of the early days in this town that a day of mourning was observed in honour of the German sailors killed when the battleship *Deutschland* was bombed by the Red aircraft.[108] Another mourning day here was for the late insurgent general, Mola, probably one of the best generals Spain has produced in modern times, killed when his plane crashed in the mountainous country to the north.

When I got to Cáceres, I was indeed very pleased to find the Fifteenth (Irish) *Bandera* there in barracks, having come down from the line they held at La Marañosa on 10 May, preparatory to going back to Ireland. In the company of some of its members, I passed many pleasant hours; I remember especially McMullen who, short of one leg, still tried to prove that there was a silver lining to every cloud, even in Spain. It was about a week before they left that I decided that I would leave the Legion.[109]

I had now been in arms for eight months; had been successively promoted '*distinguido*', '*Legionario primera clase*' and '*cabo*'. Indeed, if not in legal fact, I had been been acting-sergeant the day I was wounded, and had been congratulated by both my captain and the captain of the Twenty-Second. Certain promises regarding due recognition of my actions had been made as I was being bandaged up before leaving for hospital. My reasons for leaving the Legion were therefore, you may be sure, perfectly sound.

In the first place I had a personal grievance, in that not one Spaniard had willingly aided me in my last actual combat, either in the fight or when I needed personal help, a state of things which was absolutely inconceivable in the Legion that I had known short months before. Two of the main points of the 'credo' which was continually drummed into us were that 'under no circumstances must a wounded *Legionario* be abandoned, even if it entails the death of all'; and that 'on the cry of "the Legion to me!" the *Legionario* must immediately run to the aid, with or without reason'. Furthermore, we of the old *Tercio* always believed that our 'duty is to shorten the distance with the enemy', and retreat was undreamt of. The reason for this change in outlook lies in the fact that the old Legion officers have been killed and have been replaced mainly by *'pipi'* officers from the regular conscript army, without experience of shock-troops, to whom the traditions and romance of the Legion are non-existent, and in whom the *Legionarios*, especially the older *veteranos*, have little or no confidence. Our old officers, such as *Teniente* Ivanoff and *Alférez* Blanco, led us into whatever faced us, while this new type of officer is content to watch our progress from behind. This had a lowering effect on the men's morale, for the secret of command over men in action is not brains and spectacles but even superior bravery to what those men show. Now that the *Legionarios* were beginning to run, how long would it be before we suffered a real defeat – and if there was one thing I hated, it was the thought of being taken prisoner by the Reds, as a foreign *veterano* and corporal to boot! If Spaniards could not stand their ground – and Fascists and hundreds of others in civilian jobs were hanging about risking nothing – why should I, a mercenary adventurer, do so and risk death or capture? In the *Tercio*, there is, for example, a fatalistic objection to wearing steel helmets and we preferred our own tasseled khaki caps; but this mood which the old Legion had inculcated of itself would not stand the new conditions. In hospital, my romantic fatalism became realism.

Again, I had come safely through the decimations of the *bandera* in the University City, the heavy casualties at the taking of Pozuelo (which the enemy had said to be impregnable), and was also present at the decimation of the *bandera* on the Valencia road. Less than a dozen of those who had been in the company seven months earlier remained alive after this latest affair at Toledo, and how could I expect my luck to remain so good? I had come to Spain willing to accept fair risk of death or serious injury, but this permanent use of the *bandera* as shock-troops converted the risk into certain death, which I was not prepared to accept. For national or even strong political motives, yes; but for love of adventure at four pesetas a day, no!

Press attacks on this country also aided my decision. For instance, careful slanting of news to discredit this country, such as 'plashing' for weeks the Abdication and events connected with it, while the Coronation was fobbed off with a short announcement of a few lines the day afterwards, to the effect that it had taken place and that Italy had ignored it both officially and in the press.[110] There were deliberate untruths, such as the supposed sinking by HMS *Hood* of the biggest Nationalist warship, and stories of the 'proved' intervention by Britain on the enemy side. Articles also appeared notably one ('Mare Nostrum' in the *ABC* of Seville) which lauded the increase of Italian power in the Mediterranean and ended with a warning that a power situated two thousand miles away (i.e. Britain) had no rights therein, and that the annihilation of the then supreme Turkish fleet at Lepanto in 1571 was possible of repetition. Another nice little bit in the *'Falange Española'* was the ambitious speech of Carlos VII referring to Gibraltar again being Spanish – one little-known objective of the Spanish Falange.[111]

Readers of this book will see how, with the exception of a fortnight in December spent getting and training recruits at Talavera and Toledo, the scene of events changes smoothly and without breakage from front to front and from attack to attack. I do not say that my *bandera*'s record of such constant front line service is exceptional. It is not, for it is true of the whole Legion and only them; with the exception of some Moorish *tabors* and, to some small extent, the Carlists. I do say, however, that such constant strain on one's system is, to say the least, not good for it.

This change of mood of mine, occasioned perhaps by the depressing atmosphere all military hospitals tend to create, was confirmed and consolidated by sudden contact with the English-speaking Irishmen after my long disuse of that language, during which I had, with very rare exceptions, spoken nothing but French and Spanish. I had also met 'Tug', one of the two young sailors from the *Barham* I had met months before in Talavera, who, after several months in hospital at Cáceres spent recovering from a smashed leg, had stowed away in the Irish barracks and was going to attempt to get out of Spain with them. He and some of the Irishmen added arguments even to the extremely numerous ones that occurred to me, and so I decided that Spain would soon be a corporal less.

It was obvious that I should not get my discharge until 'the campaign' was over, possibly never, and so my only solution was desertion, a word that does not sound nice to a soldier and yet in this instance, in my opinion – although a court-martial would never have accepted my thesis – fully justified. I was soon given an introduction to the leader of the Irish *Bandera*, General Eoin O'Duffy, ex-chief of Dublin's police and a fine Irish gentleman of whose solicitousness for the welfare of his 'boys' I had heard many things. To him I am deeply grateful, even more than the subsequent aid he gave me, for his action in taking me at face value and deciding to assist me. I should not have blamed him for making excuses as to its utter impossibility, since after all he actually knew no more than that I was a Welsh corporal of the Legion attempting to desert, whose story might be true – it was, in fact – or a cloak to cover escape from the consequences of some offence or other. I first saw him in his hotel in Cáceres, and came away with a tacit promise of assistance, which meant that I could then do no more except await the departure of the Irish *Bandera* from Spain. I was now getting about on crutches, and although I knew it would be some time before I got my hospital discharge and railway voucher

'Phone: Blackrock 445.
or Office: 44458.

" Farney,"

Merrion Park,

Blackrock,

Co. Dublin.

1st. September, 19

Mr. F.H. Thomas,
16 Marlborough Road,
Cardiff, Wales.

Dear Thomas,

I am glad to hear from you again, and am very
interested in the book you are writing on your experiences
in Spain. You are quite free to refer to meeting me in
Caceres, to your request to me about getting home, to the
circumstances surrounding your leaving Spain, to any
facilities I was able to render you, to your landing in
Ireland, and to your impressions of the Brigade and its
leader.

I sincerely hope you are by now fully recovered
from your wounds. I am looking forward to receiving an
autographed copy of your book.

Yours sincerely,

General.

for the front, I was relieved when some seven days later I was told to get ready to leave at five-thirty on the morning of 17 June.

Discipline was very slack at this hospital, indeed at most of the Spanish ones, owing to the fact that there was no regular nursing staff such as one finds, or expects to find, in British, or even probably pre-war Spanish ones. Lieutenant doctors would come to inspect us about the middle of the morning and sergeant orderlies would then proceed to cleanse and rebandage wounds. During the rest of the morning girl-volunteers would do the beds, cleaners would clean the wards, and we were then left alone except at mealtimes. As a result, many convalescent patients spent nights out, appearing next morning before the lieutenant arrived about eleven o'clock. That night before the Irish left, I borrowed a walking stick and, leaving my crutches behind for the first time, went down to their barracks to sleep. I knew that no questions would be asked about my absence until the lieutenant arrived in my ward the next morning, and that even then I should probably be supposed be having 'DTs' in the town, and given further valuable hours of freedom. After a riotous night in the barracks, I went to sleep in one of the sergeants' rooms only to be aroused at 4.30 a.m., after hardly two hours' sleep. An ambulance was ready to take any sick Irishmen to the station, and in this I – in civilian suit, as were the rest of the lads, this one kindly given me by McMullen – was accordingly placed by the orders of Major O'Sullivan, commanding the Irish *bandera*. Off to the station we went and, it being perfectly light, I was figuratively on pins, as I did not know if any of the hospital staff or the Spanish interpreter with the Irish would be at the station. Having passed the station staff and got safely inside a carriage, I learnt that 'Tug' was aboard (as were some of the Spanish interpreters). The train starting, I knew that it was goodbye to Cáceres in any event, and I must say that it looked more beautiful to me then than it had ever been before!

A short journey of some four hours brought us to the frontier post of Valencia de Alcántara, where arrangements had been made for the men to be fed, at which the train came to its first halt. I knew that shortly the lieutenant-bogey of mine would be making his rounds if he had not already commenced them, and suddenly I noticed an obvious inspection of the carriages by one of the interpreters. However, in the company of Sgt-Maj. Tom Shaw, Sgt Fitzgerald and the latter's brother, who obligingly filled the window, thus blocking the fellow's view of the interior, everything cleared up nicely – as was the plate of nice chicken these kindly fellows brought me. It so happened that the search was not for me, but for 'Tug'. Several of the Spanish sergeant interpreters knew he was in the barracks but, probably through fear of a riot by the Irish, had apparently said nothing. One of them had, however, seen a chance of promotion for a spectacular arrest of a deserter at the frontier, and must have decided to look for him. He did not succeed, as 'Tug' spent the time uncomfortably lying under a seat, covered by brawny Irish legs and pieces of baggage.

At last, after an hour's stay, the train pulled out on its last few miles to Marvao, the first station over the Portuguese border. Here another problem presented itself, the obtaining of a ticket for the Portuguese train lying adjacent to ours. To get it myself meant approaching the officials in my crippled state – using a stick for the first time I was hardly able to walk. This would have drawn the attention of the Spanish interpreters to me, with fatal results, as I should have been identified as a stranger to the *bandera* and although it was now Portuguese territory, I was not going to trust the Portuguese customs officials so near to the Spanish border as that. Sgt-Maj. Shaw, however, assisted me down from one carriage and into the nearby Portuguese train, unobserved except by several conniving Irish officers. He then got me a ticket and, the Irish aboard at last, we steamed out. In the same compartment by arrangement was 'Tug' and, shaking hands, we bade goodbye to Spain and those sleuth-like Spanish interpreters, who had thoroughly succeeded in spoiling the very fine journey we should have enjoyed without their company.

EPILOGUE
On Reflection

So eight months in Spain came to an end, leaving me with a contempt for international promises, as typified by breaches of non-intervention, and with a firm conviction that for the sake of Spain's traditions, culture, religion and general well-being, Generalísimo Franco should win but for Britain's sake – and possibly that of world peace – it would be better if he lost.

1. Non-Intervention[112]

I think that by now any reader with the patience to have read the foregoing pages will realise that this policy has not been taken seriously by either side in the Civil War and that arms, munitions and men have been poured into Spain by Italy, Germany and Portugal on the one hand and and by Russia and Mexico (with the strong suspicion of the implication or tacit consent of France and Czechoslovakia) on the other.

I am not in a position to know which side first accepted or asked for foreign intervention; the first signs I saw on Franco's side were the German Junker planes which aided us to pass the Manzanares on 15 November, while it was within a day or so afterwards that I first saw or heard of any of the International Brigades on the Government side. Of the presence of Italian aid, the unsuccessful attack launched against Guadalajara by a mechanized army composed entirely of Italian men and material, speaks for itself. To the best of my knowledge no German infantry are taking, or have taken part in the war, except a small number who are purely volunteers in the Legion and, besides being split up impartially between the various *banderas*, are of relatively insignificant numbers. Franco's Tank Corps is nearly 100 per cent German-equipped and manned; while his Air Force is composed entirely of German and Italian planes. A very well substantiated rumour going the rounds among us last spring concerned the purchase of a hundred pursuit planes by Portugal from Britain of which fifty mysteriously appeared later incorporated in the insurgent forces – a fact which is impossible of denial from the evidence of sight, for on the outbreak of the Civil War the Spanish Air Force went over as a group to the government side. An exception is the seven heavy bombing aeroplanes, which were stationed with the Legion in Morocco, and utilized as air-taxis to enable the men to be landed in Spain, the Straits then being under the full control of government warships.[113] German Mausers of an old type, modern light machine-guns, munitions and artillery have also been supplied; the Spanish standard weapon has been for very many years the German Mauser manufactured under special licence in Spain, so that these matters were simply arranged. Portuguese volunteers in the Legion have increased enormously since the war began, but it is impossible to state with certainty whether by the action of the Portuguese government. New lorries of American manufacture, supplies of food, clothing and tobacco have been sent gratis into Spain by the Radio-Club of Portugal which, however, is stated to be a private organization.

Mexican aid to the Government side was proved by the capture of the *Mar Cantábrico* which failed to run the Nationalist blockade although illegally flying the British flag. This was not the first shipment of arms by a long way, as admitted in March by the Spanish Ambassador to Mexico, Señor Ordas. Russian aid was in the form of food, men, arms, munitions, armoured cars, tanks and aeroplanes. I have personal knowledge of this, especially of their tinned meat which, though partaken of as long ago as January 1937, still leaves me with a romantic sentiment. In the case of rifles, for instance, those with which the English battalion was equipped during the Valencia road operations were dated as of 1934, 1935 and 1936 manufacture.[114]

The thousands of volunteers of Czech, Polish, French, British, Russian, Argentine, German, Italian and other nationalities of the International Brigade, if in some instances free of actual intervention by the governments concerned, shows the little respect for national promises shown by the International Communist organization. The thick khaki uniforms with which they are clothed, contrasting strongly with the thin cotton clothes, more suited for African climes, worn by the *Legionario*, are also not of Spanish manufacture and is one more example of the contraband of war.

With regard to the government artillery it is claimed by the insurgents to be of Russian manufacture and mainly under the direction of French officers. As artillery never fell into the hands of my *bandera* while I was with it, I am unable to confirm or contradict this statement; but it is a fact that it is undoubtedly now of a larger calibre and handled with far greater technical skill than was the case last winter, for instance.

The assistance in manpower given to General Franco up till last spring was, according to the enemy side:

Africans of various races:	78,000
Italians:	82,000
Germans:	29,000
Irish, Poles and others:	12,000

A total of 212,000 men, of which the German and Italian strengths are probably about right, but of the rest the Irish (for example) numbered less than 700 to my own certain knowledge, while the supposed African strength is, in my opinion, a gross exaggeration.[115] In any case, this latter does not amount to intervention, as Moorish troops have always formed part of the Spanish army, and since they preferred to support Franco instead of the government the worst they can be accused of is being, like him, 'in revolt'.

The Nationalist estimate at about the same time of the Reds' foreign forces was:

Russians:	80,000
French:	20,000
Czechoslovakians:	12,000
British, Americans, Germans, Italians etc:	20,000

A total of 132,000 men.[116] The great number of foreigners acceded to the Nationalists should still leave the government forces with numerical superiority, as the commencement of the war saw General Franco with only 30,000 troops, mainly Legion and Moorish, against the 100,000 regular conscripts, most of the Artillery Corps, Air Force and Navy, and members of the militant Trade Unions, who all remained faithful to the Government.[117]

2. Internal Situation

The law and order which prevails in Franco territory cannot be denied by any fair-minded person who is acquainted with that part of Spain at the present time, although sometimes to the Legionary it seems too lawful, when one considers the hundreds of local dandies who infest the cafés without attempting to fight for their cause except by verbal means. Another sore point with both *Legionarios* and Moors are the Fascists, who boast how they will rule Spain – presumably the Legion and Morocco also – and many of whom have never yet fired their rifles with serious intent, while very few of the rest of them have been engaged in severe actions. As morally low as I consider the Communist militiamen to be, I still admire them in that they did make some attempt (albeit weak) to fight for their political principles.

With regard to outrages, I challenge anyone to prove that these have ever taken place in Nationalist territory.[118] With regard to enemy territory it is another story. Long-dead nuns were taken from their coffins and exhibited in the streets of Barcelona – a British newspaper once published photographic proof of this. Churches have been wantonly destroyed or befouled by the Spanish Government forces, by the evidence of my own eyes the churches of Navalcarnero, Carabanchel, Getafe, Boadilla, Majadahonda, Torrejón de Velasco and San Martín de la Vega; that is, places so far apart as to prove systematic destruction and not isolated instance. Prisoners mutilated – the two Portuguese of my *bandera* previously mentioned. Compulsory evacuation of women and children from their homes, hundreds of Basques, as proved by enquiries in August 1937 from Bilbao, and requests for their return. Also by an experience of mine. My exploit with the officers' cook during the Valencia road operation will be recalled.[119] His brother had been away in Seville at the outbreak of hostilities. Seville lay in Franco's hands, but his own village was in opposition country; when he was enabled to return home by the Nationalist advance, he found his wife and girl-child had gone, taken with them by the retreating enemy. The reason, I forgot to mention: he was head of the local Fascist party.

The *ante-bellum* crimes of the Spanish Popular Front sympathizers, which led to the hostilities, were the seizures by peasants of the land – a move immediately legalized by the Government; lack of control, or open sympathy with looting mobs by the police; exhumation and burning by women of the body of the Bishop of Jaca; the assassination by police officials, with the connivance of the Ministry of Justice, of Calvo Sotelo the Conservative politician. Besides, the Government was a 'packed' one, for although the election returns showed the numerical majority of the Right parties, a fresh alignment of election districts later gave the Left parties an enormous majority of actual seats.[120]

On the other hand, the Nationalists have shot prisoners also, but without mutilation, but whereas Franco has put many captured members of the International Brigade safely over the French frontier with a new suit of clothes and five pounds in their pockets, there has not been a single equivalent gesture by the Reds.[121] The latter were only restrained from shooting two foreign air pilots in Bilbao by international representations and Franco's threat of severe reprisals.[122]

With regard to desecration of churches, my *bandera* slept one night in that of Boadilla, which had been restored after earlier despoilation, but we were strongly reminded before entry that the penalty for the slightest sacrilege was death. The churches have remained open in Franco's territory, although in Madrid they were forcibly closed and kept so for thirteen months after the war began and only opened then as 'window-dressing' for foreign visitors.

I might mention that I speak on this subject without prejudicial interest, as I am not a Roman Catholic.

Again we have used some small amount of captured enemy explosive bullets, but this is only a fair retribution and has not been so consistent as the other side's use of them. The bombardment by Nationalist aeroplanes of Madrid, an immediate military objective, is fully equalled by the Red bombardment of Cáceres, Talavera, Toledo, Córdoba, Granada, Salamanca, Avila, to mention only a few of the entirely civilian centres bombed.[123]

While Franco's cause is thus to my mind the more morally justified one, yet the violent anti-British campaign run by his censor-controlled press, containing inaccuracies and even untruths, left me with the conclusion that his success will only create one more enemy for the British Empire. Moral reasons once compelled me to willingly shout '¡Viva España!' with other Legionaries; national reasons and sentiments now compel me to retract the words, without in the least implying support or condonation of the many manifold crimes of the Valencia Government side.

In conclusion, I owe many apologies for the varied use in this book of the terms 'Nationalist', 'rebel', 'insurgent' to denote General Franco's side, and 'Government', 'Red' or 'enemy' to indicate his opponents, whose seat of government is at Valencia, but take my defence in their uncertain and varied usage by the British press. Actually, for eight months, I knew them as 'Nationalista' and 'Rojo' respectively, and one would understand the use of the latter when the mottoes painted by its members on walls and churches are usually 'Long Live Russia', 'Long Live Communism (or Anarchism)'.

I feel I owe no apologies for any startling brutalities written of, for an autobiography without truth is as a clock without hands – good enough for passing the time, but without any information to be gained therefrom.

My grateful and sincere thanks are also due to General O'Duffy, Major O'Sullivan and other officers, NCOs and men of the Fifteenth *Bandera*, without whose aid I should have probably been unable to return, and who showed that no matter what the governmental feeling between our countries might be, in personal matters there is no antipathy. For the benefit of Great Britain, the Irish Free State, and the Empire generally, may that feeling continue to hold good.

Notes

1. The 'Credo' was the joint work of J. Millán Astray and F. Franco Bahamonde. Along with the examples of heroism quoted, it was extracted from J. Millán Astray's book, *La Legion* (Madrid, 1923).
2. On 'iron rations', see p. 54.
3. FHT's impressions here indicate his parochial youth. First, brought up in Sabbatarian South Wales, this was his first experience of the Latin peoples' contrasting attitude to the Seventh Day. Second, his disgust with Lisbon's 'dirty, old-fashioned trams' was influenced by the fact that Cardiff Corporation had recently established a spanking new tram system in the city!
4. A 'remittance man' was an expatriate type to be found in bars all over the continent and the British Empire between the wars. He was usually black sheep from some well-to-do family, which paid the disgraced exile a regular sum of money on condition that he did not return and renew his relatives' embarrassment. See almost any contemporary novel by Graham Greene or Evelyn Waugh.
5. 'Insurgents' was the term used for the Francoist forces by those sympathetic British newspapers (such as the *Daily Telegraph*) which sought to avoid the somehow more disrespectable alternative of 'rebels'. See also p. 130.
6. FHT's history was slightly out here. The successful Lisbon uprising against the rule of Philip IV of Spain took place in the last days of 1640. Although legal independence was not gained until the end of a long war in 1668, Portugal has always assigned its birth as a modern nation to the former date.
7. i.e., Woolworth's, still a comparative novelty in Britain's high streets.
8. FHT seems to have noticed nothing of the aftermath of the furious struggle over Badajoz, which had been stormed by the Army of Africa on 14 August after brave resistance by Republican militia units – over a thousand of whose survivors were subsequently shot. The walls he refers

to had aided the defenders, having been built to withstand artillery during the war referred to above, n. 6.

9. Since recklessness in action was (in effect) encouraged by the 'Credo', it seems that FHT's *cabo* was being complimentary, not sarcastic.

10. FHT was travelling through Extremadura, in those days a region of vast noble-owned estates (*latifundia*) and a desperately poor population, as remote from urban civilization as any colony.

11. Offering to share one's food was still the custom on Spanish trains until fairly recent years. It was, of course, one of pure politeness and its object is (strictly speaking) expected to demur gracefully. Doubtless FHT's fellow-travellers made allowances, both for his alien innocence and the wartime conditions.

12. The military Junta (*Junta de Defensa Nacional*) which had administered the Nationalist zone since July had been replaced shortly before FHT arrived in Burgos by a new government, under General Franco as Head of State. This was a (by some, unforeseen) result of the Junta's membership electing Franco as Supreme Commander on 29 September; see P. Preston, *Franco – A Biography* (London, 1993), p. 175ff. However, FHT's assessment of the Junta's president, General Miguel Cabanellas (1872–1938), was accurate. A liberal and alleged freemason, he had been opposed to the policy of terror (endorsed by both Franco and his closest rival, Emilio Mola) and distrusted Franco. The feeling was fully mutual, and Cabanellas was shunted aside to an honorific post; Cortada, *Dictionary*, p. 99.

13. The 'Big Noise' referred to here was probably the military governor of Burgos province, Gen. Fidel Dávila.

14. In his strictures upon the rail service, FHT made little allowance for the exigencies of war. In rear sectors, tracks, junctions and bridges were often sabotaged by Republican guerrilla bands, and were also attacked from the air. The narrative scenario of Hemingway's *For Whom the Bell Tolls* – derived from an actual incident – involves such an operation in the Sierra de Gredos, an area which FHT was about to traverse on his journey to the front. See (e.g.) J. Chávez Palacios, *Huídos y Maquis: La Actividad Guerrillera en la Provincia de Cáceres, 1936–1950* (Cáceres, 1994). SH had a similar experience in the Republican zone.

15. The *Falange Española* emerged in 1934 as a nationwide consolidation of various Fascistic organizations under the leadership of José Antonio Primo de

Rivera, son of the military dictator of Spain in 1923–30; see P. Preston, 'The Myths of José Antonio' in R.A. Stradling et al (eds), *Conflict and Co-existence: Nationalism and Democracy in Modern Europe* (Cardiff, 1997), pp. 159–95. Valladolid was the city of its foundation and Old Castile remained its heartland. Like the Communists, their influence in Spanish politics was small prior to the elections of February 1936. In the mounting political tension and social disorder which followed, both parties flourished; and once war began thousands of 'new shirts' joined the Falange, including many members and fellow-travellers of the PCE, who sought the protection of the blue shirt as a *'salvavida'* (lifejacket). By October 1936, *Falangista* volunteer militia represented a large fraction of the insurgent army – perhaps as much as twenty per cent. A concise description of the Nationalist army can be found in one of the 'Men at Arms' series published by Osprey; P. Turnbull et al, *The Spanish Civil War 1936–39* (London, 1978) pp. 7–11.

16. This morsel of specialist knowledge came to FHT via his later acquaintance with members of the XV (Irish) *Bandera*, who were highly conscious of the historical precedents of their mission: see pp. 118 et seq. Readers wishing to enquire further may consult R.A. Stradling, *The Spanish Monarchy and Irish Mercenaries: The Wild Geese in Spain, 1618–68* (Dublin, 1994).

17. The information supplied to FHT on this point was deliberately incomplete. The *banderas* were disbanded because of their complicity in the failed military rising led by General José Sanjurjo in August 1932; for the same reason, Millán Astray was compulsorily retired to the reserve; see G. Cardona 'La Sanjurdada: El Proceso', *Historia 16*, 76 (1982), pp. 60–7.

18. At the time FHT was writing, there were already sixteen *banderas*, and this had risen to twenty by the time the war ended; Cortada, *Dictionary*, pp. 211–12.

19. The Carlists were the 'traditionalist' supporters of an alternative dynastic claim to the Spanish throne, still technically occupied by 'orthodox' Bourbon representative, Alfonso XIII, who had neglected to abdicate when he abandoned Spain in 1931. Their support, spread across the whole of northern Spain in the mid-nineteenth century, later dwindled to a diehard sect based almost entirely in Navarre. Fanatical Catholics and violent opponents of the secular Republic, they continued to raise and train clandestine paramilitary units (or *Requetés*). In July 1936 these

volunteer militias formed the core of the insurgents' army in the north; see M. Blinkhorn, *Carlism and Crisis in Spain, 1936–1939* (Cambridge, 1975). FHT's awareness of the *Requetés*' service at La Marañosa also came from his Irish friends, who had served alongside them in this sector.

20. Like many other people of influence, Lloyd George was moved to protest by the Condor Legion's bombing of Durango and Guernica, followed by the evacuation of children from Bilbao, in the spring of 1937. These incidents, which both received saturation press coverage, called forth the last sparks of the Welsh Wizard's old magic; but it was not enough to save the dying Basque Republic. See *Spain and Britain: A Speech delivered in the House of Commons on October 28, 1937* (London, 1937). FHT's riposte may have been ill-founded in one respect – the Carlists no longer identified themselves as Basques, and use of *Euskara* in Navarre had almost died out. But, of course, many inhabitants of the Basque Provinces, marooned within a new state formally allied to the Second Spanish Republic, were supporters of the Nationalist cause.

21. The term *'quinto'* for a new recruit was not (as FHT believed) a reference to quality, but came from the ancient royal prerogative of taking every fifth man for the army from any given town or district. Traditionally, therefore, it described conscripts, but with the later use of various contemptuous slang expressions for the pressed men, the more respectable tag adhered to the volunteer *'caballero'* Legionary.

22. Under General Fanjul, the Madrid garrison declared its adhesion to the uprising. Its two main barracks (that mentioned in the text and the Montana barracks in the city centre) were cut off from one another and surrounded by inchoate militia groups after arms were issued to the people on 19 July. After short sieges, both were taken and most of the surviving officers killed; see Thomas, *Spanish Civil War*, pp. 244–6.

23. 'Picking out their spot.' Here, FHT was attempting to respect the feelings of the average reader, a customary self-censorship in 1937. In conversation sixty years later, he recalled more than once witnessing a sergeant kicking a soldier in the testicles for some real or imagined act of insubordination.

24. Both the general tone and several details of FHT's description of a disciplinary code which makes the Prussian precedent seem mild, are amply confirmed in Kemp, *Mine Were of Trouble*, passim. In an interview recorded some years later, Peter Kemp offered some remarks which may be appositely

quoted in relation to FHT's position at this juncture – though certainly the former was unaware of the latter's case. 'I'm glad I didn't join the Foreign Legion [at first]. As a private, speaking no Spanish, I'd have had a pretty rough time. I did later join them, but by that time I had my commission. Even then it was rough enough, but I did speak some Spanish by then.' Tape 9769 (Reels 1–2), Audio Department, Imperial War Museum.

25. The Portuguese were by far the largest foreign contingent both in the Legion and in the ranks of the Nationalist armies in general. (Here I except the Italian CTV, which retained a discrete command.) However, like other aspects of Portugal's contribution, this subject is still poorly investigated by historians. The official numbers reached 53,000, not all of whom were genuine 'volunteers'. See M. Roubicek, *Special Troops of the Spanish Civil War* (Doncaster, 1987).

26. FHT is now unable to recall Pierre's surname, nor the reasons which led him to disguise his identity in 1937.

27. The dramatic contrast between the legionary ranker's status inside and outside the barracks was a result of their founders' insistence on a special *'fuero'* (military privilege). They claimed this was based on the chivalric code which allegedly inspired the noble volunteers who served as infantrymen in Spain's armies during the 'Golden Age' (the so-called *'guzmanes'*). In fact, it was a version of these ideals quite as distorted as that satirically imagined by Cervantes at the time (in the mind of Don Quixote). For the weird mysticism of the *Tercio* – confused by both religious and humanistic standards – see Galey, 'The Spanish Foreign Legion', *loc. cit.*

28. As FHT implies, his cursory training reflected the desperation of Franco's commanders to fill the depleted ranks of their assault units for the 'final push' against Madrid. In normal circumstances the training of *Tercio* recruits was exceptionally rigorous.

29. For these two – 'Tug' Wilson and Yarlett – see Thomas, *Spanish Civil War*, p. 980 and n. 2. FHT was to encounter the former once again; see p. 121.

30. FHT was marginally out here. Casarrubias del Monte (in Toledo province, near the border with that of Madrid) had fallen to the Nationalists on 15 October; Martínez Bande, *La Marcha*, p. 50.

31. It was the custom to number companies seriatim throughout the whole *Tercio*, notwithstanding the Legion or *bandera* to which they belonged. In October 1936, there were three Legions of four *banderas*, each of the latter

having four companies. FHT was thus in the fourth company of the Sixth *Bandera*, and a member of the Second Legion. Further subdivisions were into *pelotónes* (roughly, platoons) and *escuadras* (squads).

32. The Italian *Corpo Truppe Voluntaria* was sent by Mussolini in response to insurgent appeals. In all, some 80,000 men passed through its ranks in the course of the war – many of them true volunteers who came to fight for Fascism, or Catholicism (and sometimes both). However, the first of these regiments did not reach the peninsula until shortly before Christmas 1936, and were not in action until the Málaga campaign of February 1937; see J.F. Coverdale, *Italian Intervention in the Spanish Civil War* (Princeton NJ, 1975), esp. p. 153ff.

The German contribution was organized in two separate commands. The Condor Legion was only the Luftwaffe squadron (and ground support). The other command comprised two artillery batteries and a small number of armoured battalions. These, too, were not fully operational until the New Year; see relevant entries by R. Proctor in Cortada, *Dictionary*, pp. 144–6. Again, many personnel were true volunteers, albeit usually inspired more by strictly military and career reasons than idealism; see the contribution by German veteran A. Lent, 'The Blond Moors are Coming!' in P. Toynbee (ed.,) *The Distant Drum: Reflections on the Spanish Civil War* (London, 1976), esp. pp. 95–7.

33. FHT admired Kozma, whose exotic origins and intellectual mien made him the ideal companion for an aspiring Beau Geste. His new friend told FHT that he had been expelled from the White·Fathers (a missionary society founded in Algiers in 1868, and dedicated explicitly to the conversion of Africa) because of an incurable interest in native women. In fact, in those days the Church did not recognize any temporal end to the sacramental state of ordination. If Kozma was not lying, he was still a priest; and his service in the *Tercio* was a characteristic example of the 'expiation' ethic it fostered.

34. In response to my question, FHT placed himself firmly in the third of his categories.

35. See p. 60.

36. In British army lingo, 'iron rations' are a cold protein-rich food supply issued to combat troops in circumstances where they are unlikely to receive support from a field kitchen. On this occasion the diet was

'chorizo' – now familiar to British palates via the delicatessen counters, but found quite inedible by volunteer Brits of 1936; see Orwell's reaction to 'that bright red sausage which tastes of soap and gives you diarrhoea', Orwell, *Homage to Catalonia*, p. 13. However, both FHT and SH were frequently issued with tinned sardines, with the difference that whereas the former hated them, according to Dannie Abse it happened to be a favourite snack of the latter. See *A Poet in the Family*, p. 27.

37. *'Seis y media'* is the Spanish version of our pontoon (i.e. originally the French *vingt-et-un*); *'monte'* is a kind of brag.

38. Given the instability of the military situation on which he had already remarked, FHT was perhaps a little unfair in this particular tactical observation.

39. The Moroccan battalions (*tabors*) were invariably launched as the first wave of any important attack. This was partly due to an implicit racism, since they were regarded as expendable colonial auxiliaries. Be this as it may, they were near-irresistible fighters, who projected fear into the minds of the most courageous adversaries; see, e.g., R. Fraser, *Blood of Spain: The Experience of Civil War, 1936–1939* (Harmondsworth, 1988) pp. 257 and 264. Selecting from numberless instances of use of this asset by the Nationalists, the most significant example is the crossing of the Manzanares on 15 November (see p. 68–9). The casualty rate among the *'indígenos'* was even higher than that of the Legion – a near-incredible 86 per cent, according to my calculations from figures given in Gárate Córdoba's statistical essay 'Los Moros', *loc. cit.*, pp. 98–9. In the circumstances it was hardly practical to deny them the privilege FHT refers to here.

40. Navalcarnero, on the main road from Madrid to the south-west and Lisbon, was before the war a large village (*pueblo*) of some 5,000 inhabitants. It commanded routes across the western and southern approaches of Madrid and its easy capture illustrated the disarray of Republican forces even at this tenth (not quite the eleventh) hour of Madrid's destiny. Indeed, the loss of Navalcarnero, after which the enemy guns could be heard in the capital, seems to have been decisive in deciding the Republican government to seek a safer base in Valencia (though most of the cabinet did not actually leave until two weeks later). However, the same event also stimulated the new *Junta de Defensa* to launch the first dangerous counter-offensive, against the vulnerable right flank of the Nationalist advance. This coordinated

operation, remarkable for the first use of massed armour in an independent battlefield role, and focused on Illescas and Seseña, developed in the last week of October. Though Franco's army needed a respite, in order to prepare its last thrust, it was more likely to have been the scare occasioned by this battle which obliged General Asensio (in the centre) to loiter on standby duty for a whole week. Aznar, *Historia Militar* I, p. 450ff; Martínez Bande, *La Marcha*, pp. 104–8; Thomas, *Spanish Civil War*, pp. 436–7, 467–8.

41. This observation was made with the hindsight afforded by the battle of Brunete (July–August 1936) in which Navalcarnero formed the pivot of Nationalist defence and recovery.

42. By no means seriously inaccurate, FHT's observations here were nonetheless influenced by partisanship. Though many did so only temporarily, later returning to seek some accommodation with the victors, the majority of the population in the direct path of the *africanistas'* advance abandoned their homes. Undoubtedly, fear of the Moroccan reputation for atrocity was a more common reason for this behaviour than explicit political opposition to the insurgents. Though referred to dismissively by Martínez Bande as *'el psicosis moruna'* (*La Marcha*, pp. 57–8), this fear was not without foundation in fact, and moreover was deliberately excited by Nationalist propaganda, e.g. the regular radio broadcasts of General Queipo de Llano from Seville. A general panic ensued, accumulating and intensifying as the enemy approached Madrid and horror stories engorged themselves with the telling. The military effect, a kind of primitive blitzkrieg, was to inundate Republican lines of communication with a tidal wave of refugee humanity flowing towards Madrid.

On the other hand, as FHT's reference to 'tender consciences' implies, the months before the insurgents' arrival witnessed a spate of atrocities against the clergy and other 'suspected Fascists' (i.e. the well-to-do), which touched almost every community in Andalusia and New Castile. Outside of Catalonia, this phenomenon was especially furious in Madrid and its provincial *pueblos*; see the analytical and statistical study by R. Casas de la Vega, *El Terror: Madrid, 1936* (Madridejos, 1995). Though most of his hard-bitten legionary comrades did not need this to lean on, FHT was able to reconcile himself somewhat to the brutalities on his own side by being mindful of these.

43. These photographs were syndicated to various newspapers in Britain and North America. See plate section. The American with the movie

camera was possibly Russell Palmer, who made the pro-Nationalist propaganda film, 'Defenders of the Faith'; this film includes some obviously 'staged' close-up action shots of a Legionary *bandera* – including one soldier who could be FHT. But it seems that Palmer did not reach Spain until early 1937. On the general issue, see Aldgate, *Cinema and History*. One of the shots taken of FHT was later utilized by Manuel Aznar in the second volume of his *Historia Militar*, 3rd edn, 1961, p. 734.

44. For the capture of Brunete, Martínez Bande, *La Marcha*, p. 75. The day's tour of duty on 29 October required covering thirty-odd kilometres in full kit and under (here, relatively light) battle conditions. But this was by no means unusual for a Legionary *bandera*.

45. At the outbreak of the war, some sixty per cent of the regular army remained loyal to the Republic, including a majority of officers. However, this force was overwhelmingly made up of national servicemen, along with many elderly and/or retired officers. Thousands of the former simply went home or joined the militias; the latter were rarely trusted by the parties and unions, many being imprisoned or shot despite professions of loyalty. See M. Alpert, *El Ejército Republicano en la Guerra Civil* (Barcelona, 1977).

The FAI (*Federación Anarquista Ibérica*) was not a trades union in itself, but the elite leadership organization of the Anarchist movement as a whole, which was popularly based on its union, the CNT (*Confederación Nacional del Trabajo*). The UGT (*Unión General de Trabajadores*) was the Socialist trades union, affiliated to the mainstream Socialist Party.

46. FHT's perception of the International Brigades as the Foreign Legion of the Republic was a natural one, and may be taken as the highest tribute he could pay them. On another level, morever, it seems a striking insight of interpretation. Of course, the Internationals were neither professionals nor mercenaries to the same degree as the Legion. But they were far more 'foreign' than Spanish in composition (at least until much later in the war); they were often well-organized and trained, highly motivated and disciplined; above all, they had few equals among indigenous regiments on the battlefield. For other compliments by FHT on SH's outfit, see pp. 94–5.

47. This was Móstoles, renowned in Spanish legend as the *pueblo*, which declared war on France at the outset of the 'national uprising' against Napoleonic occupation in 1808. Its fall was prophetic since Franco, whose

army took Móstoles on 2 November 1936, was to outdo Napoleon and succeed in conquering Spain.

48. See below, n. 56, for comment on the balance of opposing forces in the forthcoming battle for Madrid.

49. The shooting of prisoners of war was the rule rather than the exception on both sides at this juncture. Neither side had resources to spare for appropriate custody. Furthermore, the Nationalists were determined not to leave potential pockets of guerrilla resistance behind their advance, while Republican attitudes were dominated by the knowledge that they had their backs to the wall. 'Reprisals' was the accidental excuse rather than the essential reason for mutual murder. The main (not the only) difference noteworthy in the present context is the unflinching honesty of FHT's (and likewise, of Peter Kemp's) descriptions of the type of incidents which – though some certainly witnessed them – no Briton on the Republican side has ever admitted in print.

50. In the middle of this sentence FHT inserted the apparently inconsequential information that 'the theft of money from a companion being met with physical retaliation from all, although equipment, being official and not personal property, is looked upon as fair game'. The phrase is virtually a quotation from P.C. Wren's *Beau Geste*.

51. See p. 50.

52. The weapon referred to here was a crude hand-grenade of explosive packed into a tin cylinder, which resembled a modern beer can, and was set off by a similar process.

53. For murders of priests organized by trades union *'chekas'* in Carabanchel, see Casas de la Vega, *El Terror*, pp. 277–9.

54. The tank was almost certainly a T-26 – the state-of-the-art armoured vehicle which arrived in Spain in considerable numbers during October. 'Molotov cocktails' had shortly before been used by the Nationalist defenders of Seseña against enemy tanks in the narrow streets. See J. Montero Barrado, *Paisajes de Guerra: Nueve itinerarios por los frentes de Madrid* (Madrid, 1987) p. 104, and Martínez Bande, *La Marcha*, pp. 105–6.

55. FHT's unit had advanced across a section of the Casa de Campo already cleared by the Moors. Thus, it is not clear from the few sentences he devotes to this engagement that the Nationalists pushed the Republicans back only slowly and at great cost. In the six days, 6–11

November, the former suffered 2,369 casualties, some forty-five per cent of the total muster. The process took four days and nights (6–10 November) and indeed, the enemy managed to retain control of the south-east corner of the park; Martínez Bande, *La Marcha*, pp.131–6.

For nearly all the campaigns described by FHT from this point on, Montero Barrado's book (see previous note) is an indispensable aid, since it contains many photographs of defence works in their current states and topographical contexts, as well as excellent maps of the battlelines. See, in this instance, p. 25.

56. In this period (actually four days) Franco and his advisers deliberated upon and planned the final move into the capital. They realised that the enemy would mount a desperate defence, and that the imminent fighting in Madrid's streets would not offer the same opportunities as the open country which had smoothed their path to its gates. The drastic shortage of combat troops further reduced the chances of success; the last dramatic push described in this chapter was made by less than 4,000 *africanistas*, with only a few battalions of reliable troops in reserve. By the final stages of the battle, the defenders (still growing in net numerical strength) outnumbered the attackers (experiencing the reverse process) by three or four to one. Though Franco's artillery and air support was now beginning to improve, these were not decisive elements in the struggle for Madrid.

57. The Sixth *Bandera* was still part of General Asensio's column, which in turn formed the centre of three which the overall field commander, General Varela, had at his disposal for the operation. On 15 November, the battalion started from a point slightly to the north of the Royal Palace which dominates the heights above the Casa de Campo.

58. The question of supply and use of foreign equipment in the Spanish Civil War is a complex, controversial (and constantly elusive) one, and there is no space here to divagate upon it in general. (But see pp. 125–8.) However, FHT's remarks on air-power appear to contradict one expert's assertion that the Condor Legion did not operate as an integral unit until its raids upon Alicante and Cartagena – specifically aimed at disrupting Soviet supplies to the Republic – in the third week of November; R. Proctor, *Hitler's Luftwaffe in the Spanish Civil War* (1983), p. 65.

59. This building, known as 'Las Caballerizas', was first constructed by

order of Philip IV in 1625: see R.A. Stradling, *Spain's Struggle for Europe, 1588–1668* (London, 1994), p. 294.

60. The previous evening, with most of his colleagues faltering in the face of horrific casualties, Asensio announced his resolution to cross the Manzanares. During the course of 15 November, the river valley in front of the wall became littered with dead and dying from various attempts. Around 4 p.m., taking advantage of failing light, a *tabor* of the Tetuán contingent (at this point in proceedings, less than 200 men) forded the river and stormed the higher ground beyond. They found the immediate enemy positions deserted – another case of *'el psicosis moruna'*. Three companies of the Sixth *Bandera* followed quickly, fanning out to occupy nearby university buildings. FHT's company was last into the salient, and during the night they were joined by the rest of Asensio's column. For the day's events, see Martínez Bande, *La Marcha*, pp. 136–9 (from the Nationalist perspective), and R. Colodny, *The Struggle for Madrid: The Central Epic of the Spanish Conflict 1936–37* (New York, 1958), pp. 75–8 (from that of the defenders).

61. It is characteristic of extant accounts by veterans of the Spanish War that the first thought on reaching any given position should be for their stomachs and other creature comforts. *Homage to Catalonia* is often remarked upon for this refreshingly non-vainglorious feature. But FHT was ignorant of Orwell, and unlike him was writing about the climactic military moment of the whole war. Already a lot of the 'romantic adventurism' had been knocked out of him; cf. SH's similar preoccupations, below, *passim*.

62. The crudely improvised bridge across the Manzanares became known as the 'passageway of death' (*'pasarela de la muerte'*) since in daylight hours it was open to fire from enemy machine-gun nests situated some 300 yards away. It formed the unique gateway to the salient, even the Moroccans having been unable to capture any of the fixed bridges intact. (The precarious wooden structure was superimposed on the collapsed fabric of one of these.) In fact the *'pasarela'* was operational the night after the initial crossing, but since its priority was to allow the transport of men and ammunition rather than hot food and blankets, this was not revealed to the PBI.

63. The Nationalist salient was located in the vast new campus of the *Universidad Complutense*, where construction had started in the late 1920s. The Second Republic's desire to expedite completion had been hindered

by financial problems, and in 1936, several major buildings remained unfinished, most notably for present purposes the Teaching Hospital (*Hospital Clínico*) at the eastern fringe of the site. For the fighting involved in Franco's definitive occupation of this site – which he calls 'an immense collective madness' – see Martínez Bande, *Frente de Madrid*, pp. 165–79.

64. At this point, it seems probable that FHT was in the Faculty of Architecture, not that of Medicine. In collating the account which follows with those of Aznar and Martínez Bande, two unconscious lapses become apparent. First, FHT occasionally transposes the sequence of his moves from one position to another; second, he elongates the period he spent in the salient from one week to two – hardly surprising, since it was the longest week in his life.

65. FHT's booty was later lost during a rest period in Talavera de la Reina.

66. In their initial contribution, the first International Brigade (numbered XI, and mainly German) had helped to stiffen resistance in the Casa de Campo a week earlier; but (see above, n. 55) FHT missed this occasion. For their part in the new engagement, see the account in E. Romilly, *Boadilla: A Personal Record of the English Group of the Thaelman Battalion of the International Brigade in Spain* (London, 1937).

67. In this paragraph, I have slightly adjusted some of FHT's original locational references to make them consistent with historical accounts and street-plans of the area. In order to be looking down the Calle de la Princesa, his company must have been stationed to the north of the Model Prison, and not in the Parque del Oeste as such. The children's hospital was probably the Asilo Santa Cristina, which fell to the Sixth *Bandera* on 17 November; the 'house down below us' probably the Dr Rubio Research Institute. FHT remembers at one stage being in the main Teaching Hospital contested over four days of intense close-quarter fighting. Once captured, this building constituted the furthest loop of the whole salient.

68. In conversation, FHT remembered that before a regular food supply was established, he found some stale bread in one of the buildings, which he wolfed down with relish. Various Republican sources relate that Moroccans in the *Hospital Clínico* ignorantly killed and ate laboratory animals, many shortly dying of diseases thus contracted. The story is intended to illustrate the incongruous and destructive relationship of Franco's 'savages' to the world of modern science represented by the

Republic. More significant, if mundane (and if true), is that it points up Franco's callous indifference to the food supply of his loyal Moors.

69. The mass murder of right-wing prisoners was little known about outside Spain until the 1970s, and FHT's (perfectly accurate) reference to it here would have occasioned at best puzzlement and at worst derision had his book been published nearer the time of writing. On the nights of 7 and 8 November some 1,500 victims were taken from the Modelo to two villages, Paracuellos del Jarama and Torrejón de Ardóz, to the east of the capital, where they were machine-gunned and buried in mass graves. See two contrasting but equally fascinating accounts issued by the same Barcelona publisher in 1983; I. Gibson, *Paracuellos – Como Fue* and C. Fernandez, *Paracuellos del Jarama – ¿Carrillo Culpable?* José Antonio was tried and shot in Alicante (not Málaga) on 20 November.

70. Relevant to points in this paragraph is a grisly incident recalled by FHT during our discussions of the fighting in the University City. Execution was the normal punishment for being found asleep on sentry duty, though, as in the case of Shostek, men were too valuable to waste at this particular juncture. One night, FHT found himself nodding off at his post, and could do nothing to forestall the inevitable. Then he heard the awful screams of a militiaman who had been captured by the Moroccans, who was being tortured in a building somewhere behind him; the sound kept him awake for the duration of his two hours duty.

71. In this chapter, FHT's chronology conflicts with that of the experts. One of the latter dates the aborted last offensive, across the Parque del Oeste, against the Model Prison and Don Juan Barracks, as 20 November; Montero Barrado, quoting the memoirs of the Republican general, Vicente Rojo, (*Paisajes de Guerra*, p. 26). Another fixes it as 21 November; Martínez Bande, *La Marcha*, pp. 142–3: and a third as a day later still; Hills, *The Battle for Madrid*, (London 1976), p. 105. In another place, Martínez Bande states that on (or around) 21 November 'the Fourth *Bandera* relieved the Sixth, which was totally expended'; *Frente de Madrid*, p. 177. All agree that on 23 November, eight days after the Manzanares crossing, Franco, after conferring with Mola and Varela, called a halt to the battle for Madrid; see, e.g., Thomas, *Spanish Civil War*, p. 487.

72. '*Vivandières*' (a euphemisim annexed from *Beau Geste*) equals 'camp followers'. FHT's belief in innocent ways of contracting syphilis was not

unusual (even among soldiers) in this period, and it hardly invalidates his criticism of the doctor.

73. Boadilla has a special resonance for anyone with an interest in the Spanish Civil War. The village had been taken by the Nationalists a week before FHT's arrival, in the engagement after which Esmond Romilly's book, arguably, after Orwell's, the best-known individual memoir of the conflict, was titled; see above, n. 66.

74. On the Romanian volunteers, see *Los Legionarios Rumanos Ionel Motza y Vasile Marin, Caídos por Dios y España* (Madrid, 1941), which confirms FHT's details. The two men named in the title of this pamphlet were killed within a few days of this encounter at Majadahonda, where a memorial commemorates them; Montero Barrado, *Paisajes de la Guerra*, p. 66.

75. The religious destruction lamented here is replicated in accounts from both sides; dozens of members of the Irish *Bandera* (XV) recorded similar details of various *pueblos* of the Jarama sector in the early months of 1937. Moreover, the specific incident described in the next paragraph was also by no means unique; see my forthcoming *Crusades in Conflict: Ireland and the Spanish Civil War* (Manchester, 1998). FHT cannot now recall by what means he recognized the holograph of Philip II. Spanish kings usually signed the famous '*Yo el Rey*', but often their names appear on documents written in Latin, of which this appears to have been an example. The eighteenth-century palace at Boadilla was built for an *infante* of the Bourbon dynasty.

76. This was the beginning of 'the battle of the Corunna road', the first stage of Franco's new plan for gaining Madrid by cutting it off from the outside world and starving the capital into surrender. These operations, taking place mainly west and north-west of the city, were also aimed at mopping up all the open countryside outside the built-up area. The stage objective was attained with the cutting of the road to Galicia, but stout resistance in the foothills of the Guadarrama mountains around El Escorial frustrated further progress.

77. Female members of the militias were recalled from the front a few months later; Fraser, *Blood of Spain*, p. 286. In conversation, FHT revealed that treatment of this prisoner was not actually Quixotic at all, but rather followed a less exclusively Spanish custom.

78. The meaning here seems self-contradictory.

79. '*¡No Pasarán!*' had now, of course, become as much the universal slogan of

the Republic as '*¡Arriba España!*' was of the Nationalists. On the various battles for Pozuelo, see Montero Barrado, *Paisajes de la Guerra*, p. 64.

80. Despite the vulnerability again illustrated by this incident, the Republican forces continued to place great faith in the efficacy of armoured trains, which was preached in various section magazines of the army; see, e.g., 'El tren blindado. Su relación con otras armas y servicios en la guerra' by J.J. Ganose, *La Voz del Combatiente*, 17 March 1937. This piece celebrated the successful use of the weapon during the battle of Guadalajara. To some extent it was seen as a substitute for cavalry of which the Republic had a serious shortage.

81. In a rare mistake, FHT renders this awkward place-name as 'Majahoanda'.

82. See pp. 50–1.

83. I.e., the forward look-out position in any given section of a trench.

84. The Emperor Charles V (Charles I of Castile and Aragon) died in 1558 at the monastery of Yuste in Extremadura.

85. For the population of Valdemoro, this blissful interlude was about to come to a volcanic end. The artillery which FHT had spotted was a battery of German 88-mm guns, which was seeking to install itself nearby in readiness for the new offensive. The town, also used as the distribution centre for the forthcoming battle, soon became a major target for enemy guns and aviation.

86. In conversation, FHT joked that although he felt sorry to be left behind his companions, he would have been even sorrier to have been in front of them – i.e., one of the opposition.

87. The action described in this chapter shortly became known to history as the battle of Jarama. FHT's unit joined the engagement on its sixth day (11 February, his own reckoning being one day out) and was withdrawn from the line shortly before it finally subsided into a stalemate (22 February). The Sixth *Bandera*'s temporal and topographical experience of this combat was thus the exact equivalent (as it were, from the other side of the mirror) as that of the British Battalion of the XV International Brigade against whom (*inter alia*) it was directly pitted.

88. The bridge was captured on the night of 11 February (while FHT slept) by a party of Moroccans who crept up on the guards and knifed them to death; Thomas, *Spanish Civil War*, p. 589. But the enemy facing Asensio's column at this stage did not belong to the International Brigade. A similar operation had taken place that morning at the Pindoque railway

bridge, a few kilometres north. Here, the bodies were examined by Peter Kemp, then a *Requeté* officer, who confirmed that they were French (members of the André Marty Battalion of the XIV International); see, Kemp, *Mine Were of Trouble*, pp. 71–2.

89. On the morning of 12 February, Asensio's units came up from the river onto the Sierra de Pingarrón, advancing along both sides of the road to Morata. Simultaneously, the XV International Brigade was moving towards them head-on. On the ground, at least, both sides were largely ignorant of the immediate situation. His scouts and runners may have alerted Aranda Mata; and (for his part) XV Brigade C-in-C, Col. Copic, may have been able to question Spaniards who had retreated from the heights. However, all the evidence suggests that the Sixteenth (British) Battalion, which had only arrived that morning in lorries from Chinchón, and were facing their first action, had little or no idea of what they were about to experience.

The Sixth *Bandera's* field of action was to the north of the road, where they quickly routed the Fifteenth (Franco-Belgian) Battalion and later also pushed back the Eighteenth (Balkan or 'Dimitrov'). Both in terms of numbers and terrain their task was somewhat easier than that on the other side of the road, where a Moroccan *tabor* had been sent to capture the crucial hilltop of Pingarrón itself.

See Bill Alexander, *British Volunteers*, pp. 94–102. A more extensive treatment of the battle will be found in my forthcoming *Crusades in Conflict*.

90. Bitter argument over use of dum-dum and impact-explosive ammunition will probably never become capable of resolution, so, rather than burden the reader with another reading-list, I will leave FHT's side to speak for itself on this rare occasion.

The *Mar Cantábrico*, chartered by the Republic and loaded with *material de guerre* from the USA and Mexico, was captured by the Nationalist navy in March, 1937.

91. Non-partisan sources confirm that at this stage of the battle, the skies were dominated by Republican (i.e. Soviet) fighters, though things in this respect became more even in the last stages of the struggle; see, e.g., Thomas, *Spanish Civil War*, pp. 589–90.

92. FHT's sequence of events here seems slightly awry. I cannot explain his two days of comparative inaction, since furious counter-attacks were now the order of the day from a constantly reinforced enemy. The bayonet

charge he witnessed can only be that made on the evening of 13 February by members of the British First Company in a desperate attempt to rescue comrades of the Second (Machine-Gun) Company who were captured by Moors around 4.30 p.m in a position about 400 yards south of the road.

93. Gen. Wrangel was one of the counter-revolutionary (or 'White') leaders who, backed by various Western powers, attempted to crush the Bolsheviks during the Russian Civil War of 1919–21.

94. FHT added an appendix to this tale. He was informed of Kozma's death by two men of the platoon who came to see him some time later, bringing a memento which the dying man had willed him. They told him about the explosive bullet. The memento was later lost with most of FHT's other effects at Talavera. When he got home, FHT wrote a letter of condolence to Kozma's family, via the latter's uncle who was foreign minister of Hungary at the time.

95. It seems possible that these men were members of the machine-gun company (see previous note), since there is no record of another group being captured. But from the information they provided, and the very fact of their providing it, they are more likely to have been individual deserters, and from a later point in the battle. NB: there was no 'Anglo-American' unit; two separate battalions of Americans (with some Irish) and British (also with some Irish) took part in the Jarama battle.

96. As the following sentences (perhaps unconsciously) betray, 'El Tercio' had met its match for the first time at Jarama; indeed, the last offensive actions of the battle, referred to here, were being made by the enemy, above all, the Lincoln Battalion, on the heights of Pingarrón. See Montero Barrado, *Paisajes de la Guerra*, pp. 94–6.

97. El Pardo is one of several royal palaces in the vicinity of the capital. Previously a hunting lodge, situated in a desolate area north of Madrid, after the war it was selected by Franco as his personal residence. As FHT suggests, his new billet was on the southern boundaries of its enormous estates.

98. In August 1936 a Legionary *Bandera* had been formed on Majorca, to help repulse a Republican landing from Catalonia. This particular threat was soon ended, but it was still some time before most of its members could feel assured of the security of their island; at which point some were transferred to the mainland. See J. Pérez Vengut, *Porto-Cristo, el Legionario y otros heroes* (Palma de Majorca, 1937).

Such was the need for men willing to risk their lives in the *Tercio*, that known ex-Anarchists captured from the militias (as well as criminals and other desperados) were now being incorporated, at least into the new *banderas* of the *Tercio* (VII–XVII); R. Kern & M.D. Dodge, *A Historical Dictionary of Modern Spain, 1788–1988* (New York 1990), p. 216.

99. There were no Russian troops in the International Brigades and no Soviet combat units (as such) with the Republican fighting forces. Individual Russians served in the Brigades as senior staff officers, political commissars, or technical support aides – or with the airforce as fighter pilots. See Alpert, *Ejército Republicano*, esp. pp. 251–7.

100. This site was one of dozens, scattered throughout territory remaining loyal to the government, where insurgent supporters sought refuge during July 1936. Most were soon overcome. However, Santa María de la Cabeza, situated on a remote peak of the Sierra de Morena, was a more difficult target – though equally difficult for the Nationalists to relieve. (FHT seems to have slightly advanced the date of final capture, which took place in April.) For a concise account, Thomas, *Spanish Civil War*, pp. 630–1. In Francoist myth the tale achieved a heroic profile second only to that of the Alcázar, and a feature film was made about it ('¡El Santuario no se rinde!') in 1949.

101. FHT thus arrived in Villanueva, which was to be the scene of SH's death, at exactly the time that the latter left Cardiff for Spain.

102. Around this time, FHT noted down, in pencil, on a page of his notebook which has survived, the unit-relationship of his escuadra and the relevant names:

Sexta Bandera, Comandante [vacant]
24o Compañía, Capitán Núñez [crossed out] – *Ruis*
3a Sección, Alférez Rodríguez
2a Pelotón, Sargento Matilla

3a Escuadra, Cabo Frank Howard Thomas
        Legionario 1a Clase Julián Fernández Sánchez
        do   *Antonio Barrera Carmona*
        do   *Antonio López Martínez*
        do   *Francisco Suero Bejarano*
        do   *Martín Lorente Adán*

103. See p. 60.

104. The engagement which FHT now describes goes unrecorded in the specialist volumes cited. In contrast it receives full treatment in the memoirs of Enrique Líster, who was in command of the Republican troops engaged; see *Memorias de un luchador* (Madrid, 1978), p. 224ff. To some extent these things are explained by the fact that the battle was a Republican victory – though one with no strategic consequences.

The front line established in October ran very close to Toledo on the east and south. In an attempt to obviate potential dangers, on 7 May the Nationalists began an advance towards the village of Polán. Twelve kilometres of No-Man's-Land and a small enemy-held village were taken before serious opposition built up. Líster's crack 11th Division was rushed to the scene, and in a week's bitter fighting, the Nationalists were pushed back to positions closer to Toledo than when they started.

No International Brigade forces were involved in the action, which actually demonstrated the growing maturity of the Popular Army and its indigenous regiments. On the other hand, the assumptions made by FHT represent another tribute to the former. Líster confirms other details given here, e.g., the important role played by Republican tank battalions.

105. The *bandera* was moving through the foothills of the so-called '*Montes de Toledo*', a relatively modest sierra in terms of size and height, by Spanish standards, but more impressive than anything FHT had seen at close quarters before.

106. [Note by FHT, detached from text.] 'The Moorish troops are organized in two categories; as *"regulares"*, from the coastal districts of Morocco, with mainly Spanish officers and training; and the entirely Moorish *"mehalla"*, from the interior. The latter, speaking only Arabic are fully mercenary auxiliaries, fighting for Spain when the prospects of pay and loot are good, and against her if prospects by doing so are better. As a result, they are unstable, being better than the *regulares* while in a victorious advance while not so hesitant about retreating if hard pushed.'

107. The scars of the wounds FHT sustained on 10 May 1937 are clearly discernible today (along with that of the dreadful wound in his back made by a piece of German shrapnel five years later). The face wound was caused by a bullet ploughing its way along his cheek, apparently without actually entering the mouth.

108. The German navy exacted a ruthless retribution for what was the

result of a crass blunder on the Republican side. On 31 May a squadron led by the *Admiral Scheer* bombarded the defenceless port of Almería for almost two hours, causing nineteen civilian deaths; Thomas, *Spanish Civil War*, pp. 685–6.

109. For the Irish *Bandera*, see my 'Franco's Irish Volunteers', *History Today* (March 1995), pp. 40–7; and 'Battleground of Reputations: Ireland and the Spanish Civil War', P. Preston and A. Mackenzie (eds), *The Republic Besieged: Civil War in Spain 1936–1939* (Edinburgh, 1996) pp. 107–32. Both are preparatory to more detailed treatment in my forthcoming *Crusades in Conflict*. Tom McMullen was injured by sniper fire on the Jarama front. He features in a press photo, taken on the *bandera's* return to Dublin, and reproduced in the plate section.

110. The abdication crisis developed after FHT had left the country. Edward VIII abjured the throne on 12 December 1936 and the new king, George VI was crowned on 25 May 1937.

111. Editions of *ABC*, Spain's monarchist daily, appeared simultaneously in Madrid and Seville. After July 1936, the former naturally supported the Republic, while its *Sevillano* brother took the other side.

From this point FHT, a supporter of British Monarchy and Empire, became increasingly resentful at the revival of traditional anglophobe attitudes in the Nationalist zone. The latter developed in response to the fact that, after the bombing of Guernica (a propaganda disaster from his point of view) Franco lost the public support of many elements in British public life. In the battle of Lepanto, a key event of Spanish-Catholic history, the infidel Turk had been driven back from the 'Catholic' Mediterranean. Only Gibraltar gave some assurance that even worse might not befall Britannia – and the Rock was now being threatened, as this revival of a speech made by a late Carlist Pretender ('Carlos VII', d. 1909) illustrates.

112. For this and what follows on the perennially debatable statistics of intervention, the most recent assessments are summarized in M. Alpert, *A New International History of the Spanish Civil War* (London, 1994).

The foremost expert considers that Britain's record was rather the opposite of the impression given by Francoist propaganda; see E. Moradiellos, *Neutralidad Benévola: El Gobierno británico y la insurrección militar española de 1936* (Oviedo, 1990).

With his usual care for detail, and influenced by a growing detachment,

FHT succeeds in avoiding an utterly misleading survey. (We must remember that his data comes from public sources in Spain and Britain available in mid-1937.) Certainly, his persistent reference to 'the government side' and occasional use of 'the insurgents' suggests a certain resistance to some of the basic and imperative assumptions of the Francoist movement.

113. This item is gleaned from a story aimed at asphixiating the truth about the initial (and crucial) Hitlerian intervention, the supply of twenty Ju 52s, enabling the bulk of the Army of Africa to cross the Straits of Gibraltar in July–August 1936; see A. Viñas, *El Alemania Nazi y el 18 de Julio* (2nd edn, Madrid, 1977). However, about a third of the total force did reach Andalusia by other means.

114. Despite the sedulously preserved myth that the International Brigades were always badly equipped (as well as out-numbered) many veterans confirm (usually *en passant*) the use of Russian weaponry which was modern and effective. The British Battalion, for example, was issued with new automatic rifles in the week before the Valencia road battle (i.e., Jarama). Of course, at later stages of the war, both supply and distribution of Soviet material were intermittent and unreliable.

115. Oddly enough, the figure for Moroccan troops given here is identical to that arrived at by Gárate Córdoba as valid for the whole war, and the same goes for the Italian CTV; see Córdoba, 'Los Moros', *loc. cit.*, p. 98, and Coverdale, *Italian Intervention*, p. 417.

The other two figures are very wide of the mark. No more than 4,000 Germans served in Spain. FHT's figure for the Irish contribution is almost exact. Poland may have been associated with the Nationalists *via* assumed religious affiliation, but evidence suggests that a mere handful of Poles fought for Franco, compared to over a thousand in the International Brigade. On the other hand, French volunteers were numerous enough to form two companies ('Juana de Arco') in the XVII *Bandera del Tercio*.

116. As previously stated, the Russian presence here is pure fiction, a key part of Nationalist mythology. The others are perhaps not quite so far divorced from reality, especially if for 'Czechoslovakians' we read 'East Europeans and Balkans'. As it happens, a veteran of the XIII International Brigade, mostly made up from Slav battalions, is also now living in Cardiff – George Nowaczek, who was born in Czechoslovakia, but emigrated to

South America, and came to Spain from Argentina; see *South Wales Echo*, 18 July 1996.

117. Though FHT has a point here, his estimate of the total Nationalist resources at the start of the war is very conservative, and the government advantages were mainly on paper; quantitatively dissipated by the social revolution; qualitatively crippled by lack of experienced commanders; and (in the cases of airforce and navy) technically disabled by want of material supply.

118. Given FHT's candour about the brutalities he observed on both sides in the battle zones, and his admission of the efficacy of Nationalist propaganda (see below), the blanket refusal here to accept that outright atrocity was a mutual phenomenon is a little surprising. The issue is far too intense and complex to broach in this book; my own thoughts on it will be found in 'The propaganda of the deed: History, Hemingway and Spain', *Textual Practice 3* (1989), pp. 15–35.

119. See p. 96

120. In this paragraph FHT rehearses various points put forward by Nationalist propaganda, laying the blame for the violence and disorder, which (allegedly) led to the Civil War, on the Republic, and justifying their cause by denying the legal legitimacy and moral authority of the Popular Front government elected in February 1936.

121. The only instance of such magnanimity known to me (*sans* suits and *sans* cash) was the freeing of the British volunteers captured during the Jarama battle, after several months of harsh imprisonment, in April 1937.

122. This refers not to captured combat pilots, but to the idiotic exploits of the pro-Franco British playboy, Rupert Belville; see V. Cowles, *Looking for Trouble* (London, 1941), esp. pp. 99–100.

123. Corroboration of FHT's assertions is called for here, if only because English language textbooks consistently elide the simple fact of air raids on open cities made by the Republican airforce. However, it was the latter who initiated the tragic sequence, with their attack on Granada in July 1936, while Cáceres was raided (100 victims) a few weeks after FHT left; for comparative data, see P. Vilar, *La Guerra Civil Española*, 5th edn (Barcelona 1992), p. 152.

An open page from SH's diary:

THE DIARY OF
SID HAMM, 1937

NB: *Asterisks appearing alongside names and places indicate the failure of editorial attempts to identify them.*

Sunday, April 11th

Pat Sloan★, (evening). Youth Group Rumble. Left Theatre.

Monday, April 12th

Group.

Friday, April 16th

Spanish Aid Committee.

Saturday, April 17th

Left Cardiff for London 12.15. Left London for Paris 8.20.

Sunday, April 18th

Arrived Paris 5.30 am. Left Train 7.00 to *L'Humanité*. Nothing national. Found 'Red Cafe'.

Monday, April 19th

Rita fetched us to *syndicat* in Rue de la Vallette. Mooched round Paris. Nearly drowned. Left for Seté 9.05 pm.
[Russ★ sent back][1]

Tuesday, April 20th

9.35 am Seté. One group lost. O.K. Arrived HQ. Family Hotel. Police. Bed.[2]

Wednesday, April 21st

Moved to HQ. Eat, drank, smoked, played cards. Walked.

Thursday, April 22nd

As above.

Friday, April 23rd

As above.

Saturday, April 24th

As above to 12 noon. Meeting. Eat at 5. Boarded schooner 8. Left for Barcelona.

Sunday, April 25th

Cruise in night. Two red planes and 'flying' boat H63 TBD off Barcelona. Arrived 5.50. Kept waiting on quay. Taken to Anarchist Barracks. Organization all to hell.[3]

Monday, April 26th

Up at 6.30. Breakfast at 8. Coffee and bread. Hung around 'till 12. CP Headquarters. Grand old Church. Decided to go on to Valencia 6.40 p.m. Had look round Barcelona. [illegible phrase]

Tuesday, April 27th

5 am Not far from Valencia. Not bad trip. No rations. Arrived Valencia 5.30 pm. Messed around. 7pm no accommodation. 7pm food. 9.30 train Albacete. Hell of a trip. No sleep. Sardines.

Wednesday, April 28th

Arrived 11.30 am. Signed up. Grub. Outfit. Left for Madrigueras. Arrived 4 pm. Headquarters. Grub. Mooched round. Bed fairly early. Too cold to sleep. Woke every now and then.[4]

Thursday, April 29th

Up 5.30. Coffee + bread 7 am. Free to 8.00. Rifle instruction. Grub. Sing-song. Cold.[5]

Friday, April 30th

Field manoeuvres. Automatic rifle. Cold.

Saturday, May 1st

Dug ditch. Grub. Rifle instruction. Fiesta. Warm day, cold night.[6]

Sunday, May 2nd

Reorganization. 3rd American. Moved barracks. Rest.[7]

Monday, May 3rd

Reorganization. 1st British. *Muchos bueno*. Meeting. Liaison and cultural. Meeting – cultural.

Tuesday, May 4th

1st manoeuvres with British. Bayonet and marching. Afternoon, bomb instruction, Ted Bramley.[8]

Wednesday, May 5th

Field manoeuvres. Attack. Talk by comrade back from front. Range instruction. Lecture, Ralph Bates.[9]

Thursday, May 6th

Manoeuvres. Defence. Talk by Thomson, American Commander. Wall newspaper set up.[10]

Friday, May 7th

Field manoeuvres. Hellish hot. Rest in wood, afternoon. Cultural meeting. Nothing new.

Saturday, May 8th

Field manoeuvres. Defence. Medical. Counter-attack. Rest. Played football, age plus or minus 19, Spanish Company. Won 2–0.

Sunday, May 9th

[illegible phrase] Foot started aching.

Monday, May 10th

Field manoeuvres. Defensive. Retreat. Attack. Hellish hot. Complimented on manoeuvre. Slept most of afternoon – indoor inspection.

Tuesday, May 11th

Training in field use of automatic rifle and grenade. Lecture by Mexican on night attacks, pretty good. Fried eggs at Matilda's. Paid 75 pesetas.[11]

Wednesday, May 12th

Due for guard. Couple of hours L.P. Back to barracks. Lounged round. Built fireplace – pretty good. Feed of steak and chips. Took over guard 6.30 p.m. Went sick 8.30. Orders to sleep all night. Missed guard.

Thursday, May 13th

English comrade back from front attached himself to us. Reported sick. Had foot seen to. Dry dressing. Pretty sick. Went to doc, evening. Foot poisoned. Pretty bad. Went straight to bed. Langmead arrested. Drunk and disorderly.[12]
[Bought scarves, Albacete]

Friday, May 14th

Company reorganization. Section 3 turned up, Bill Morrisey etc. Met G. Nicholls. Field telephone. New barracks. Not bad. English lecture. Enjoyed myself. Wrote articles for Iskra. Sick. Foot lanced. Pretty bad, bilious etc. Missed inoculation. Met Miles Tomalin.
[Gale back with games, Albacete][13]

Saturday, May 15th

Sick. Indoor instruction on machine-gun. New issue of Iskra. Formation of class begun. First Spanish class. Food terrible.

Bellyache all night. Discipline tightened up – about time. Langmead returned. Met Hugh Slater.[14]
[Spanish class good. Boys enthusiastic. Keeps them out of the gin swills]
[reprimanded by commandant][15]

Sunday, May 16th

Sick. Lounged about. Wrote home, Jack⋆ and Joe⋆. Talked to new comrades. Lot of tripe. No grub except bread, milk, fruit and lettuce. Stomach pretty bad, foot improving. All shops shut. Wrote home. Talk by Doc. Short of soap.

Monday, May 17th

Sick. Improving. Had news leaving for front. Got permission to go. Fixed it OK. Wrote Leo. Dinner. Paraded in full kit. What a weight. Left Madrigueras 3.00 pm. Trucks – Albacete. Train at Albacete. Had grub. Beef, bread, water, oranges. Cold. Fell in outside train for Lorenson⋆. Slept but up 5.30 am.[16]
[Met a Spanish comrade. Officer, ex-railway worker. Had a long talk with him, followed by sing-song.]

Tuesday, May 18th

Good wash at Aranjuez. Breakfast, as tea, without oranges. Tried to make coffee. Diluted tinned milk. [illegible phrase] Good strawberries and peaches. Lovely women. Picked up by trucks around twelve. Up to Brigade Headquarters. [illegible]. First experience of fire. Shell and rifle. Down to English headquarters. Tea. Good sleep.
[Jarama front, XV Brigade, English. Had long talk with Jock Cunningham.][17]

Wednesday, May 19th

Up late, 7 am. Bread, butter tea. Cleaned rifle. Lounged till 10.30 – up to front. Started to march. Lorry was hell. Met Alec Cummings, OC Company! And – yawn – met Pat Murphy again, Alec's dug-out. Food, bread, soup, mush and peas, rice pudding, cherries. Grand. Tea, bread, butter and cheese. Good sleep. [illegible phrase] [Fired first shots. Fixed rifle.][18]

Thursday, May 20th

Going guard duty 4 am–6 am. Cleaned rifle. Breakfast. Built dug-out. Read and slept. Doc inspection operation. Grub. Soup or nothing. Rained like hell, tea time. Bedtime read, sing-song. Due for parapet work. Too wet. Slept fairly well.

Friday, May 21st

Up about six. Breakfast. Greased cartridge. Canteen open. Sweets and fruit. Wrote Gerry. Lecture by Ralph Bates on new government. Pretty good. Wash. Bit of digging in dug-out. Good grub all day. Concert in evening, guitars and singing. Sounded great, lovely night. Slept well. 5.30 diarrhoea. Heel dressed. Mail from mother.[19]

Saturday, May 22nd

Breakfast. Cleaned rifle. Diarrhoea better. Saw Doc. Foot improving. Teeth on leave. Dinner. Hellish hot, no water. Mule shot in leg. More digging. Moved to new dug-out – bags. Company runner refused order. Sacked. Alec Cummings arrested. Had stand-to with rifles and gas-masks, appear to expect something. On guard 2–4. Pretty good. Frost* reckless, plenty of firing.
[8.30 pm false alarm. Second guard duty – 5–6 pm. Slept well.][20]

Sunday, May 23rd

Breakfast fatigue 6 am. Stand-to. Heel dressed. Ears. Bought sandals from John Kelly. Wrote Leo and Bert. [illegible] of guitars. Paid 70 pesetas. Decided to be home by September. Met Lance. Talk by Jock Cunningham. Met Pitcairn. Comrade Graham on England. No mail. Wrote Leo. Night off. No fags. Late night.
[Saw Will Paynter, said it would be OK about going home.][21]

Monday, May 24th

Breakfast. Cleaned rifle. Stand-to. Wrote articles. Yarned. Cleaned dug-out. Read most of day. Section meeting on leave etc. Slept. Sing-song. Went to bed early. Very hot. No mail, no fags. Guard duty 12–2. Bed.

Tuesday, May 25th

Breakfast. Diarrhoea. Cleaned rifle. Slept and read. Stand-to. Foot dressed. Diet. Slept and read. Tea. No envelopes. Grand sing-song. No guard. Two W.D. (1/23rd). No mail.

Wednesday, May 26th

Bread butter and cheese breakfast. Stand-to. Foot dressed. Wrote home, Gerry.

Thursday, May 27th

[Blank]

Friday, May 28th

[Blank]

Saturday. May 29th

Saw Doc. Wangled bath. Could buy nothing in Morata. First set shorts issued. What a relief. Guard. Canteen restocked, mainly beer. No mail.[22]

Sunday, May 30th

Fired 30 rounds to keep enemy in trenches. Lounged round for rest of day. Guard. Had photographs battalion taken. No mail.

Monday, May 31st

Breakfast, stand-to. Dug trench, played cards. Read book. Bombing party proposed. Did not volunteer. Complete balls. Was informed I was in party about 8.30. Refused. Party cancelled. Enemy appeared to know about it. Guard 10–12. Bed. Wrote home. Saw photos Cardiff Docks.

Tuesday, June 1st

Breakfast. No money. Read books, lounged about. Spent most of day in Tom's dugout. Guard 8–10. Wrote home. Letter from Mother. Guard 12–2.[23]

Wednesday, June 2nd

Grub fatigues. Played cards. Bath afternoon. All shops closed in Morata. Rained at tea time. Bed early. Rained all night. Lousy. Cold. Issue of 10 Woodbines, Spanish chocolate.

Thursday, June 3rd

Guard 2–4. Rained. Cold. Stand-to. Paid 77 pesetas. Played cards, won about 60 pesetas. Good concert in Tom's dug-out. Bed about 10 pm. Rained, but mostly fine. No mail.

Friday, June 4th

Breakfast. Dug trench. Wrote home. Dinner. Played cards, tea. Cards; won about 100 pesetas. Letter from Hilary★. News of Mola's death.

Saturday, June 5th

Guard 4–5. Breakfast. Played cards. A.S. Read. Grand concert. Foulkes M D 2. Letters Leo, Mother; cig. lighter from Leo. Wrote Hilary. Bed. Up at 2, mistake in guard, wasn't on.[24]

Sunday, June 6th

Talk, Ralph Bates. Dinner. Played cards. Not so well, ached all over. Rained like hell. Very short rations. Wrote Mother, Leo. [Comrade X] appointed Company Political Commissar, Pat Murphy Section Political Commissar. Alec Cummings was refused transfer to Machine-Gun company.
[Given letter to reply to papers, etc. No mail. No guard.][25]

Monday, June 7th

Grub fatigues. Lecture by Copeman. Machine-gun fire. Road shelled during grub fatigues. Anti-tank firing. Dinner (6 pm). Maggots. Thrown away. French command brief. Guard 10–12. No mail. Wrote Alice Muchmore★, mother and Joan★. Rained at intervals.
[Saw Aitken, political commissar, in front line for first time][26]

Tuesday, June 8th

Grub terrible all day. Hell of a row. Entire change of cookhouse. Jack Williams in charge, Bevan★ down there. Rained like hell. Lousy. First rumours of leave. No mail, didn't feel like writing. Bed fairly late.[27]

Wednesday, June 9th

Breakfast, bread, butter, cheese. Sandwiches for lunch. Dinner lousy. Colics and diarrhoea. Foulkes got off with 10 days labour. Bloody lucky. Weather lousy, rained like hell. No mail, bed early.[28]

Thursday, June 10th

Guard 12–2. Talk by Copeman [illegible] gramophone. Cleaning up prior to moving out. Wrote mother, Leo. Foulkes missing. Fine am. Letter from Leo. Grub fairly good. Guard 8–10. Lost 75 pesetas.

Friday, June 11th

Grub poor. More rumours of leave. Pretty bad, colics and diarrhoea. Weather fine. Back in shorts. Men thinking of leave, or would have been, but not over dinner. Foulkes, on guard, nearly shot one of own men. Yarn in trenches. Definite news Red★ died. Letters from mother and Ted. All is very good. Issue 5 English cigs. Bed early. Night very cold.[29]

Saturday, June 12th

Grub fatigues. Heard going out tonight or tomorrow. Packed kit. Wrote home and Leo. Played solo and read. Ward killed by trench mortar. Pretty nasty. No sleep. Grub pretty bad. No mail. Fine.[30]

Sunday, June 13th

Guard 12–2. Quiet. Copeman round 1.15. Roused men to move out. Left on guard. Eerie sensation – alone in trench. Met at cookhouse. Breakfast. By camion to Mondéjar. Lousy. Saw it all in 10 minutes. Grub terrible. Drunken swine. Slept out. Great. No mail.

Monday, June 14th

Grub fatigues. Battalion meeting. Hot air as usual. Paid 70 pesetas. Bought beret. Lounged about. Mail from Bert, Kath*. Diarrhoea and wind. Grub bad. Started to write to Bert. Not too good. Went for walk with Steve*. Cold night, hot day.

Tuesday, June 15th

Sick parade. To Morata for dental treatment. Great time. Dinner, chocs etc. Picton sent prison, drunk. Pity. Rest battalion route march. Row about it. Wrote Bert. Hot day, cold night. Slept with Lance's company. Eggs for supper. Picton in clink. No mail.[31]

Wednesday, June 16th

Due to have lecture by Klaus*. Postponed till tomorrow. Lounged about and read for rest of day. Walk with Steve after supper. No mail. Foulkes sent to Jerry Battalion. About time. Terrific row about drunkenness. Discipline should be enforced.[32]

Thursday, June 17th

Klaus didn't arrive. Sick. Diarrhoea. Very bad. Ears being treated. Read most of day. Canteen open. Sweets, cigs etc. 50 pesetas. Great concert with Madrid artistes. Good dancing. Reynolds* going home. Letter from Mrs A.[33]

Friday, June 18th

Sick. Rifle inspection due. Polished up the rifle. Inspection did not take place, typical of disorganization. Washing returned, 10 pesetas – expensive. Lazed during afternoon. Wrote mother, Leo, Ma Abse, K. Doyle★. Well that's over. Due to play football in evening. Lousy. Back to camp. Supper of bread, tomatoes and beer. Letter from Gerry – 10 Players.
[Brigade UGM. Bit of a row because men ignored.]

Saturday, June 19th

Sick. No parade. Rifle inspection. Bathed. Wrote Gerry in afternoon. Lazed and read. Sick. Walk with Lance in evening. Glorious night. Back for supper and bed. More drunkenness. Hot. No mail.

Sunday, June 20th

Much the same programme. Drunks everywhere. No discipline. What an army. Officers just as bad. Cream of the working class. Jack Williams in hospital. Pretty bad. Hottest day yet. No writing. No mail.

Monday, June 21st

Sick. Parade. Route March. Boring. Visited Jack Williams. Read most of afternoon. Hot. Played football in evening. Strained back. Pretty good game. Will Paynter up. Brought candles, etc. Bed early. Not too well. No mail.

Tuesday, June 22nd

Sick. Back and diarrhoea. Marched to bullring for speech by Tapsell. Copic didn't turn up. Pollit down. Letters Leo and Lou★. Row because

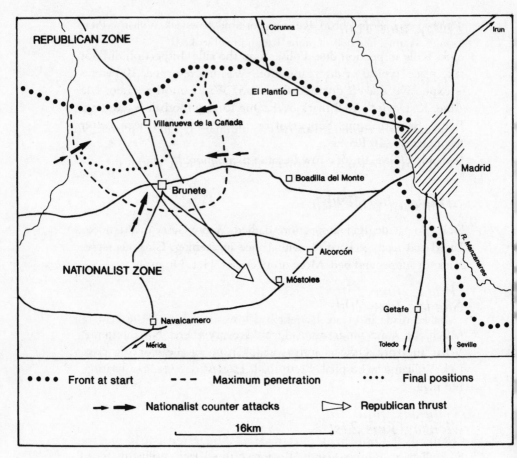

The battle of Brunete, July 1937.

of first news about Bilbao. Read rest of time. Saw Jack Williams. Pretty rough. Rained like hell all night. Kit and mail soaked.[34]

Wednesday, June 23rd

Still raining. Felt pretty bad. Copic due. Still waiting. Impromptu concert. Went running with Alec Cummings. Cleaned up later. No mail.
[Had to run for Coca★ to bring bedding etc. Pretty bloody.]

Thursday, June 24th

Not too well. Played cards, 70 pesetas-odd up, 300 in wallet. Not bad. Letter Phyllis★. Wrote Phyllis, Leo, Ted, Dora. Bed early.[35]

Friday, June 25th

Mistake made in bread. Bought bad loaves. Grub bad. Breakfast not too good. Anti-typhoid injection. Pretty sore. Ached all day. Half bath. Sick. Parcels very good – 70 cigs and mags – pamphlets, etc. Didn't sleep too well. WD. Pretty good English summer. Wrote mother.

Saturday, June 26th

Funeral of Quinlan. Court-martial. Suggested battle meeting instead of impromptu concert. Hell raised over Bilbao etc. Copeman lost temper. Not too well. Supper out – eggs, chips, milk. Good. Blood drunk – 10 days pay stopped. Anniversary of love affair. No mail. English summer weather.[36]

Sunday, June 27th

Grub fatigues. Arms inspection. Wrote Leo and Lou. Letter from Phyllis. Very amusing. More drunks, including Blood★.[37] No sign

?Daniele Week now. Beer in canteen. Nothing else. Walked round town. Discussion with boys on organization and talks with Mick U* and Graham.

Monday, June 28th

Reveille hour too early – 6 am. Complete balls-up. New order of day given out. Informed of revision Spanish army tactics. Returned to billets 4.30. Overton court-martialled. Guilty. Stripped and prison. Trial looked like a raw deal. Aitken, Copeman, Cunningham acted according to Graham. News from Brigade. Letter from A M*. New order introduced. R.600 Gym 6.30–7.00. [Tom Davis goes home.]³⁸

Tuesday, June 29th

Up 8 Breakfast. 8–9 meeting. 9–9.30 Overton stripped. 9.30–11.30 meeting for reorganizing section. Not enough present. Company meeting. Theoretical instruction. No one woke me, so slept till 5.30. Talked Alec Cummings and cleaned rifle. Fucked it up. New Battalion orders in.

Wednesday, June 30th

Reveille at 5.30, Breakfast 6–6.30. Parade 6.45. Route march and manoeuvres with gas mask. Seems serious. 8.30 to Madrid – teeth. Arrived Madrid, 12.30. Lunch. Stroll round. Back to dentist, 4 pm. Nothing done. Friday due back. Bought 'Grey Dawn'. Fixed up with Alfonso for 3 pesetas per night. Grand time. Dinner in Gran Via for 3.70 pesetas.

Thursday, July 1st

Great coffee and bread. Out shopping, 41 pesetas on books, 125 on camera. Hell of a to-do. Fixed it. Lunch at Alfonso's 3 pm. C.P. Hotel. Cinema – 'Merry Widow' in Spanish. Bought new shawl - Early blue bitter, 40 pesetas. Hotel John. Sick. Supper. Read. And so to bed. Some news of camion going back.

Friday, July 2nd

Coffee and bread. Walked to dentist. Due back for lunch 3 pm. Walked back. Pretty good. 'Top Hat' in English. Grand. Back to Velazquez. Up to barracks.[39]

Tuesday, July 6th

[Entry by ? John Williams]
On this day Sid Hamm was killed in Brunete, Spain.

Notes

1. *L'Humanité* was the French Communist Party daily. Here SH and his group received instructions. ['Nothing national' is obscure.] At the 'Red Café', they evidently found the guide, 'Rita'. My suspicion that this was the codename used by Charlotte Haldane, was confirmed by another member of this group, Lance Rogers, with whom SH was later to become friendly. Haldane acted as liasion officer for British volunteers with the French Communist Party. At the cafe, the group was split up. The cloak and dagger set-up was supposed to perplex the *Gendarmerie*, who sporadically sought to apply the strict requirements of the Non-Intervention agreements. If such a policy was rigorously in force, one imagines that even Inspector Clouseau would have been able to pinpoint the offices of *L'Humanité* and the *Syndicat* (Trade Union) Headquarters. However, the 'Red Café' *was* actually raided; Rogers, who had stayed there, was arrested as a vagrant and kept in jail for two weeks. As the next entry suggests, he was not alone in this fate; See, *Western Mail*, 20 February 1996.

[Material printed in square brackets represent snippets of extra information recorded by SH in the 'Memo' section of the open-page diary, and are nearly always separately dated by him. I have been unable to identify 'Russ', who had, it seems, misbehaved in Paris.]

2. Seté was a frequent transit point for the volunteers at this stage of the war.

3. Given the explosive situation obtaining in Barcelona at this point in time, it seems likely that the group was actually under detention by the CNT – even being held as hostages. If so, the anarchists released them after negotiations with the PSUC the next day. SH was disturbed by this experience, which possibly even began his disillusionment.

4. Albacete was the base and HQ of the International Brigades as a whole. The training camp for the British Battalion of the XV Brigade was located some fifteen kilometres to the north, in the village of Madrigueras.

5. As this entry demonstrates, military training began immediately upon arrival; the following days reveal a programme that was both comprehensive and rigorous. This gives an impression only rarely encountered in other sources.

6. SH's ditch digging was, clearly, entrenchment practice.

7. The arrival of large numbers of Americans had necessitated the formation of a new Battalion (19th, 'Washington'). But many of the newcomers were Canadians, so a third North American battalion, later known as the 'Mackenzie-Papineau', came into existence. To accommodate them, the 16th (British) was moved to premises in the nearby *pueblo* of Tarazona de la Mancha; P.N. Carroll, *The Odyssey of the Abraham Lincoln Brigade: Americans in the Spanish Civil War* (Stanford, California, 1994), p. 126; B. Alexander, *British Volunteers*, p. 72.

8. Alexander (ibid., p. 106) states that Bramley, London District CP Secretary, came to Spain on a political visit, but this entry suggests that he made a specific military contribution.

9. Ralph Bates was a British Hispanist, novelist and intellectual who became editor of the Brigade magazine *Volunteer for Liberty*, and was a constantly active propagandist for the Brigades and the Republic.

10. There were two Thompsons in the Lincoln Battalion, but this was probably Robert, later to be leader of the US Communist Party; see Carroll, *Odyssey*, p. 253 and passim.

11. 'Matilda' is also remembered by Fred Thomas, who arrived in

Madrigueras a few weeks after SH. 'Once, and only once, a few of us were tipped off that there would be eggs at Matilda's cafe that evening for first comers. . . . We all paid heavily for such unwonted dissipation'; *To Tilt at Windmills*, p. 21. All the same, the cash amount specified here refers to SH's service back-pay, not the cost of the meal.

12. This is the first of what was to become a regular series of complaints. SH was clearly not a drinker, and was perhaps oversensitive in this area. He preferred to save and spend his money in other ways; oddly, his successful gambling at cards aided this pursuit considerably. Like SH, however, the errant Langmead was to die at Brunete; see Alexander, *British Volunteers*, p. 269.

13. Morrisey and Nicholls were fellow-Cardiffians; see my *Cardiff and the Spanish Civil War*, pp. 102–3. Miles Tomalin was another intellectual comrade, active on the cultural side of things. *Iskra* ('The Spark') was a Comintern magazine, founded by Lenin – evidently SH was taking his duties as cultural officer seriously at this stage. Comrade Gale was a brother of the West Wales party activist, Tom (see Francis, *Miners Against Fascism*, p. 37) and seems also to have been mobilized in the task of providing alternative entertainment to the bottle.

14. Hugh Slater, commander of the anti-tank battery, and later Brigade Staff Officer, was also an intellectual, keen on catering for the perceived cultural deprivation of most of the volunteers. His efforts were not always appreciated by the rank-and-file; see Thomas, *To Tilt at Windmills*, esp. p. 55.

15. SH neither dates, nor gives a reason, for this clash with authority.

16. 'Leo' is Leo Abse, active supporter of the Spanish Republic at home, later to be Labour MP for Pontypool, and one of the foremost social reformers of his generation. 'Lorenson' seems to be some senior Brigade officer, unidentified.

17. Jock Cunningham, one of the heroes of the Jarama battle, was a senior CP official and ex-army sergeant, later promoted to Brigade Staff.

18. Alec Cummings was a Rhondda man who, after service in the Welsh Guards, settled in Cardiff. At this time he was OC of the 2nd Company, to which (it seems) SH had been allotted, and was later killed in the retreat from the Ebro (1938). On Pat Murphy, see Stradling, *Cardiff and the Spanish Civil War*, pp. 92–4. There is a hint here that SH was not too impressed by the loquacious and politically maverick Irish-Cardiffian.

19. 'Gerry' (Dooley) was a comrade of SH's in the Cardiff Communist student circle.

20. As the bracketed phrase indicates, the incident leading to the arrest of Cummings was one of the regular 'scares' mounted by both sides. Later material reveals that the intriguing reference to teeth means that SH will get dental treatment when he goes on leave.

21. SH's decision to apply for repatriation was reached after only one week at the front. Perhaps it was a result of his poor state of health, but other factors, and especially a limited sense of commonality with his comrades, clearly contributed. His intensifying homesickness can be gauged by the number of letters home he is now writing – after no mention at all of such a pastime down to 11 May. Will Paynter, the South Wales Miners' leader, was doing a tour of duty as Base-Camp Political Commissar at Albacete; see his autobiography, *My Generation* (London, 1972), pp. 61–81. Around this time he told Pollitt that 'repatriation is the big question for us. Every day there are new demands. I am getting as hard-faced as an undertaker': letter of 20 May 1937, IBA Archive, Box C/13/5.

Lance Rogers had now caught up with the men with whom he had left Cardiff. A miner's son (born Cefn Coed, Merthyr, 1916) he remembers SH fondly. They were two of the youngest Welshmen to go to Spain and got along well. But Lance, one of eleven children, had the feeling that SH 'had a bourgeois background which was different to ours'.

Bert Greatorex was a close school friend of SH's at Howard Gardens. 'Frank Pitcairn' was the nom-de-plume of the *Daily Worker* reporter Claud Cockburn. 'Graham' may be Frank, the Sunderland student who has since edited and published much documentary material on the Brigades.

22. Morata de Tajuña, a few kilometres behind the lines, was the only *pueblo* within walking distance of the trenches in this part of the front. As such it was the headquarters of various Spanish units and any supplies reaching village shops would soon be pounced on by officers and their batmen.

23. 'Tom' is, perhaps, Tom Adlam, from Pentre (though it could equally be Tom Picton, see below, n. 31).

24. The code coming in to use here (see first use 23 May) seems to refer to drunken states and/or associated bad behaviour among comrades.

25. The events in this entry are obviously connected, but the name of the new Company political commissar to whom Cummings objected is

indecipherable. SH had (meanwhile) been detailed to write to the home press on some topical issue, and given a list of standard/appropriate phrases for this purpose.

26. George Aitken was XV Brigade political commissar.

27. Jack Williams, Dowlais, was one of the older volunteers, and died of an illness contracted in Spain within a year of returning in 1937.

28. It should be noted that disruptive behaviour did not necessarily imply bad soldiership. For example, both Pat Murphy and 'Taffy' Foulkes behaved courageously in action. On the latter, who distinguished himself at Hill 481, see *Volunteer for Liberty*, vol. 2, no. 32, pp. 8–9.

29. 'Ted' is Ted Edwards, whom SH partnered in a memorable debate at Cardiff Technical College when, in a propaganda campaign, a 'student team' from Nazi Germany toured the university cities defending the Third Reich against its critics. Edwards later became the first Vice-Chancellor of Bradford University.

30. R. Ward, from Manchester, is recorded as having died on the Jarama front around this time in B. Alexander's 'Roll of Honour' (*British Volunteers*, p. 275).

Apart from a few days at Alcalá de Henares in April, the battalion had been in the line for more than four months. They were now given a break at the village of Mondéjar, in the higher reaches of the Tajuña valley. But this respite only came because the Brunete offensive, in which its members would be needed as shock-troops, was already being planned.

31. Tom Picton, a volunteer from Treherbert in his fifties, was later to be shot for persistent insubordination by the Francoist authorities at the POW Camp of San Pedro de Cardeña, Burgos, in 1938. He is the only drunk for whom SH shows any sympathy.

32. The 'Jerry Battalion' was the punishment battalion of the Brigade, similar to the *'pelotón'* described by FHT, where serious sins were expiated (see pp. 106–7).

33. Mrs A = Mrs Abse, mother of Leo and Dannie.

34. Wally Tapsell, Assistant Battalion Commissar, was killed in Aragon in March 1938; Colonel Copic, a Yugoslav Communist, was C-in-C of the XV Brigade; Harry Pollit was secretary-general of the CPGB.

35. The letter to Dora Cox mentioned here is extant as part of the Coalfield Collection of the University of Swansea, and is reproduced on page 176. Subject to the normal censorship – unlike this diary – it gives a

S.R.I, Playa de Altozano 161
Alboreti, Spain
25th June 1937

Dear Dora,

I have just seen your letter to Jack Williams and was immediately struck with a fit of penitence in which I am scribbling this to you. I don't apologise for not having written before since I hate writing anyhow, & also I thought that Bill Morrisey would keep you informed. Anyway I know you will be pleased to hear that I have put you on my 'once a week' list. The others are Leo Abse, Gerry, mother and now yourself. The others I write to as I get the letters.

You probably know all the news from Jack. We arrived Alboreti 28 April & went straight to Madrigueras. There, for some unknown reason I was made Cultural Leader, a job which now, Thank God, I have got rid of. I never did like work anyway. After about 18 days there we proceeded to the front. It was amazing! In the morning we received news that we were leaving for the front at 2 p.m. Immediately all the patients left the hospital, some against doctor's orders, the cooks left the kitchen against orders, the hospital orderlies downed tools & in fact everyone who could hobble or crawl was on parade to go to the front. I've never experienced anything like that before, & believe me was an emotional sensation I shall never forget. Why, about a week after we reached the front a boy we had left in hospital arrived. He had left hospital against orders & tramped & 'hitch-hiked' his way to Jarama, about 70-odd kms.

While we were in Madrigueras we had lectures by Ralph Bates, James Ford, Bob (?Hunter), Cashman, (illegible) & dozens of others such as the Doctor. The most amusing part was the cinema show. First it was silent & like an old time 'Hickie". It was not continuous & between the reels a 'chairman' got up & made a speech which we all loudly applauded, not knowing what the hell it was about, but 'when in Rome do as the Romans do'. Our other amusements were football, drinking 'cafe leche' (coffee & milk to you) (when we could get it) & buying and eating fruit. Not a very strenuous life you say? That of course we only did during the evening. The morning & afternoon were taken up with route marches, attacks on hills over open country, counterattacks & lectures on military strategy. All this under a blazing sun (quite poetic) we bore willingly, knowing that we were luckier than those who had gone before, in that we got any training. And so, when the time came to fight, we were ready & eager (This tale I will continue in my next. I must keep something to write about).

Jack is down sick here. I don't know what it is, but I hope that it's not serious, although I must say he looks very rough. Anyway the Welsh boys here are looking after him, for he's a great comrade.

I end up on my usual appeal for Players, Chocolate and reading material especially magazines & light novels e.g. Penguins. Well, I'll say au 'voir now, Dora, & will write regularly in future.

Revolutionary greetings to Lewis, Len, John, little John, Gwen, Mrs Aubrey, yourself, etc etc - Sid.

P.S. Bill M(orrisey) is at Madrigueras, Nicholls is in the field telephone (company), Price & Alec Cummings & Pat Murphy here. Bill Coles is dead (more of that later). Find enclosed our paper & some Spanish fags. If you can stand those your TUFF - Sid.

(Source: Swansea University Library, S.C. 167)

Notes:
Dora Cox, the recipient of this letter, was at the time serving a sentence in Cardiff jail for taking part in violent disturbances during a B.U.F. rally in Tonypandy in 1936. James Ford had been the Vice-presidential candidate of the U.S. Communist Party in the election of 1932. Most of the other names mentioned are comrades associated with SH's political life in Cardiff. For further information, see my *Cardiff and the Spanish Civil War*, and H Francis, *Miners against Fascism*.

Letter from Sid Hamm to Dora Cox, 1937

almost diametrically different impression of his experiences and attitudes, full of sweetness, light and political solidarity.

36. According to Alexander (*British Volunteers*, p. 273) the Irish volunteer, Maurice Quinlan, was killed at the battle of Jarama in February. This was corroborated in the list compiled by M. O'Riordan in his *Connolly Column* (Dublin, 1979) p. 163, and has very recently been reiterated in detail by Quinlan's fellow Waterford comrade, P. O'Connor, in *A Soldier of Liberty* (Dublin, 1996), pp. 17, 42. Though he clearly writes 'Quinlan', SH must therefore refer to Frank *Quinton* of London. This volunteer is recorded by Alexander as dying in action at Morata in June 1937. SH's diary suggests – all but explicitly – that he was executed as a result of a court-martial, presumably for desertion.

Bilbao fell to the Nationalists on 19 June, which meant the loss of huge industrial and population resources to the Republic. The feelings of Fred Copeman, formidable commander of the British Battalion, were both understandable and typical.

37. Blood was not (however) an accompaniment to the meal described in this entry, but rather the surname of another bibulous comrade.

38. Bert Overton, in command of the Fourth Company, panicked during the battle of Jarama, and pulled his men back without orders, allowing the machine-gun company to be enfiladed with many killed or captured (see p. 148). However, evidence of courage in earlier battles caused many men to be equivocal about his case. Eventually, a list of other misdemeanours was added to that of cowardice, and he was duly convicted. Overton was killed at Brunete working in a punishment battalion; see Alexander, *British Volunteers*, p. 107.

Tom Davies of Bedlinog returned home on compassionate grounds because of the serious illness of his mother; Francis, *Miners Against Fascism*, p. 168.

39. SH spent his all-too-brief leave in a small hotel run by the Communist Party. The barracks referred to was also a CP institution. It was formerly a convent, which had been emptied of its former denizens and requisitioned for use by the famous 'Fifth Regiment', in what had been a wealthy quarter of Madrid; see D. Mitchell, *The Spanish Civil War*, p. 196. On Friday 2 July, SH left the barracks by lorry, presumably travelling directly to the lines north of the city, whence in his absence the XV Brigade had moved preparatory to the forthcoming offensive.

INDEX